Theology's
Strange Return

Don Cupitt

scm press

© Don Cupitt 2010

Published in 2010 by SCM Press
Editorial office
13–17 Long Lane,
London, EC1A 9PN, UK

SCM Press is an imprint of Hymns Ancient and Modern Ltd
(a registered charity)
St Mary's Works, St Mary's Plain,
Norwich, NR3 3BH, UK
www.scm-canterburypress.co.uk

British Library Cataloguing in Publication data

A catalogue record for this book is available
from the British Library

978 0 334 04372 0

Originated by The Manila Typesetting Company
Printed and bound by
CPI Antony Rowe, Chippenham SN14 6LH

Theology's Strange Return

Contents

CONTENTS

Introduction

'I cannot forgive Wittgenstein', said a philosopher-friend of mine, 'for his view that there is nothing beyond culture.'

I call this view of Wittgenstein's 'radical humanism'. It's a view that has reached us as part of the long-term legacy of the work of Kant and Hegel. It is the view that 'life' – that is, the going-on of things in the human life-world, the world of language, the world of history – has no outside. The only world we have and can know is *our* world, a world seen always and only from our own perspective and in the light of our own theories. Everything is immanent, contingent and (in a broad sense) *human*. Our theories about the evolution of stars, for example, may be more or less well grounded and defensible; but we can no longer claim to know that they are *ratified* by anything quite independent of the human world. Knowledge is no longer to be seen as something that comes down to us and is given to us: it is something that we make for ourselves. Culture has entirely swallowed up Nature, so that nowadays there is indeed 'nothing beyond culture', and our knowledge does not have the old kind of objective anchorage. Everything – our religion, art, politics, morality, natural science and history – is produced and remains suspended within the movement of our own ongoing human exchanges, which means that the traditional metaphysical sort of philosophy that sought absolute knowledge has now been almost entirely replaced (at least, among the avant-garde) by the philosophy of language and the history of ideas. There is no absolute Beginning of things, and there will be no concluding revelation of the Final Truth; there is only the end-less conversation

vii

of humanity. That's radical humanism, and successive major philosophers since Kant and Hegel have been gradually grasping and stating its implications more and more clearly. And remember that I don't want you to conclude that our world is only our dream: I'm simply pointing out that it is *our* world, real enough for us but without any independent corroboration.

If to question all established forms of authority and to try to gain a better understanding of things by starting from nothing and on your own is to be a humanist and a critical thinker, then of course there has been within the Western tradition a strand of humanistic, critical thinking ever since the first stirrings of philosophy. In an analogous way, there has been a strand of humanistic, critical religious thought in the Jewish and, later, the Christian traditions ever since the Hebrew Bible was written and compiled. But the decisively 'Modern' turn, away from traditional and objective authority and towards the human subject as the starting point for thought, begins much more recently. In religion, it starts in the early fourteenth century with Wycliffe, Huss, the *devotio moderna* and the mystical writers of that marvellous century. In literature, it starts especially with Erasmus (*c.* 1500), and in religious thought it starts especially with Luther. In physical science and cosmology it begins with Galileo, and in philosophy it begins above all with René Descartes and his method of universal doubt.

Which philosopher was the first clearly to understand that the turn to the human individual subject as the starting point for all thought was a turn to time, to transience and to a kind of subjective consciousness that must simply accept as a fact of life the realization that it cannot look to any extra-human endorsement to support it? Who, to put it with entirely appropriate crudity, first saw that from now on we are on our own? Alone, really alone. I think there's a good case for saying that the young David Hume, in the early 1730s, got it about right intellectually and felt its full force emotionally.[1] Since his time we have pushed the whole argument a little further by replacing sense-experience with language as the basic currency of thought, and by decentring the human self even more thoroughly than Hume himself did. But the basic realization – that from now on, we are on our own — has been clearly implicit ever since the foundation of modern natural science by Galileo and Descartes. Today, the whole culture presupposes that we are on our own: for example, not even Church leaders claim that climate change and its consequences are simply a matter for prayer and repentance. We must *deal* with them, and do so on our own.

Why? Because modern natural science was, like modern philosophy, from the first based on the *questioning* of the claim that Truth already exists out there, being embodied in an intelligible, eternal Order of Reason, or in the Divine Mind, or just in Tradition. From now on, we are not just *receiving* knowledge from something outside space and time that already possesses the fullness of it, as if we are looking for help to something that already knows, and itself *is*, the Answer. No, from now on human beings are going to have to see themselves as the only makers of their own knowledge. And that is true not only of empirical knowledge, but also of religion, ethics, art, politics, law, and the rest. Everything is in language, everything is in time, everything is human, corrigible, secondary and constantly changing. All our knowledge is improvised *bricolage*. It seems so *weak*: but of course our modern knowledge is at the same time vastly *stronger* than the old sacred knowledge.

From this we can see that the fully developed postmodern nihilism that so alarms ordinary people nowadays was already latent in the Modern turn to the human subject half a millennium ago. Science is, and was from the first and long before Darwin, implicitly atheistic. The novel is, and was from the first, implicitly atheistic. Postmodernity and Modernity are coeval: they have always overlapped. *Tristram Shandy* (1760) is more perfectly postmodern than *Robinson Crusoe* (1719) is modern. The entire Modern period, since the later Middle Ages, has been a long drawn out rearguard action, a struggle to delay the full impact of the postmodern condition that is now everyone's everyday normality. The Modern age has been a period of overlap between the old 'heterological' kind of thinking favoured by religion, and the 'autological', critical kind of thinking whose reign in every subject is the defining characteristic of the modern university.[2] But now that long and interesting period of overlap is ending. Old-style 'belief in God' is at long last in sudden and final collapse.

By a final irony, we human beings have at last come to ourselves just in time to recognize that we may be about to extinguish ourselves. A strange position to be in. I am often reminded now of Michel Foucault, prematurely on his death-bed, and I think of my own discomfort at having to admit at the end of my life that I have backed such a collection of lost causes. But who hasn't? Nowadays we all of us end our lives thoroughly disillusioned – and yet glad to be so. It will be the same for you too, in time.

So much for radical humanism: *empty* radical humanism, because the self has of course died too, now. Everything is just a beautiful, empty fountain of signs, pouring out and rushing away. Before long the light may be going out, not only for each of us individually, but for all of us collectively, too. The *Divine Comedy* has turned out to be a comedy of the absurd, and it will end with a black page.

Now I have a question. If we cannot avoid the conclusion that there is nothing beyond culture – that there is only the humanly appropriated world of 'life' – does any possibility of religion and a religious attitude to life remain to us? I am not here talking about 'fundamentalist' religion, which is so counter-cultural, so hysterically anti-intellectual and of such poor quality that it scarcely deserves the name of 'religion' at all, being perhaps better seen as a form of paranoiac right-wing nationalism struggling to defend a previous, but now-threatened, communal identity. No: fundamentalism is of no intellectual or religious interest at all. What we are presently to discuss is the well-known fact that the whole culture remains strangely pervaded by religious art, religious language and religious feeling. Even though we *know* that there is not literally any God, nor life after death, nor supernatural order, nor anything 'absolute' and eternal, yet we still remain temperamentally religious beings – indeed, as much so as ever, as is shown by our continuing to yearn after a whole variety of 'impossible' love-objects.

I have written about our impossible loves elsewhere.[3] Here we broach a fresh topic: we are to describe and discuss the curious way in which major themes of standard religious doctrine are not merely persisting, but undergoing transformation and coming back to us in postmodernity. I'm calling this 'Theology's Strange Return', with the idea of reminding the reader that in the old Gospel narratives describing the appearances of the risen Christ, Jesus returns in a strange, transfigured form that makes him hard even for his followers to recognize. Our purpose is to investigate how far this idea can be taken. Is a new mutation of Christianity in particular, and perhaps of some other traditions also, now beginning to take shape within our Empty-radical-humanist culture?

I'm so concerned about my own utter failure hitherto to make my own ideas clear, that I propose now to give much of the plot away at the outset with a few examples.

Consider, first, the old 'theological' notion that the world is ordered, shaped, formed by the power of language. In Genesis 1–2.3, at God's word of command primal Chaos is divided up into the various cosmic regions and shaped into a world ready for habitation by the first human beings, so that Adam and Eve come to themselves in a complete ready-made world, like a furnished house with everything already running for them. And this world is so much a world already shaped by language that at least until the seventeenth century, and also in other traditions such as Islam, people continued until Early Modern times in one way or another to see the world as a world of signs, and Nature as a Book that must be read aright. John Dryden (1631–1700) still makes noisy entertainment out of the old world-view, even after the rise of Modern science. God's Word of command has something of the power of music:

> When Nature underneath a heap
> Of jarring atoms lay,
> And could not heave her head,
> The tuneful voice was heard from high:–
> 'Arise, ye more than dead!'
> Then hot, and cold, and moist, and dry,
> In order to their stations leap,
> And music's power obey.[4]

Dryden, a generation younger than Milton, is writing in 1687. He is living in the age of Newton and the Royal Society. His Aristotelean Catholicism is all over, and the triumph of the new mechanistic determinism has ended the hitherto popular idea that because Nature was originally formed by language, we can best understand Nature by reading the signs of the times – that is, by a literary interpretation of it. After Newton, English literalism cannot see language as doing any more than just *copy* an independently real world. Language no longer creates.

But then, after Kant and Romanticism, and especially after the turn to language in early twentieth-century philosophy, the old idea of the creative power of the Word returns. The world is being continuously made and remade by the ever-changing language in which we all of us describe it and the theories under which we view it. Whereas God was formerly seen as having made the world once and for all by his own commanding utterance, we now see *ourselves* as being through our own conversation among ourselves the only makers and remakers of our own world. The world is well adapted to be our habitation because *we* have made it so. We *must* make it so: one can scarcely imagine human beings constructing a picture of the world as being quite uninhabitable by them. On the contrary, in postmodern thought there are no ownerless worlds: every world is *someone's* world, his own life-world. Language and experience, words and things, I and my life-world always belong together.[5]

Thus in postmodernity the ancient mythico-religious idea that language shapes the world returns in a new radical-humanist form.

A second example: God in the Bible makes the first human beings 'in his own image', and a long tradition in the Bible and subsequently urges human beings in one way or another to imitate God's faithfulness, mercy, etc. What does this mean? How are we now to understand the odd fact that for thousands of years we have in one way or another believed the empirical world to be created, known and controlled from a hidden supernatural world beyond it? Why did human thought have to take this route in order to develop?

An answer that increasingly suggests itself, and was indeed entertained by the young Hegel,[6] runs as follows. The earliest humans, having very little theory, had little or no chance of being able to understand and control either wild Nature, or indeed themselves. Those who first acquired language and tried to think the human situation were utterly overwhelmed. They could cope only by imagining that there were greater invisible beings who could and did understand and control both the human psyche and the world. 'I can't make sense of it, but I have to believe that there is a larger perspective within which it all makes sense.' By serving and communicating with the spirits one might hope to win their protection, and even gain a little of their powers. The entire history of theology, from the dawn of humanity down to the rise of Islam, the last and at its height the grandest of all the old religion-based civilizations, is a story about how we slowly developed our ideas of sovereignty, of dominion and domain, of a law-governed unified cosmos, of the moral law, and of a unified, morally accountable human self. All these ideas (and more) could only be developed *via* theology – that is, by heterologous thinking. Only with the help of God could we gradually, gradually become ourselves; for all along there was *also* the idea that God would progressively transfer his glorious powers and attributes to us. The human being was all along destined to be God's deputy, God's agent, God's vicegerent, the crown of creation, Anthropos, the cosmic man, the Microcosmos. Thus it is true, even from a radical-humanist standpoint, that God has created us in his own image: for it is through the idea of God that we have gradually been able to become all that we now are. Thus we can and should still be grateful to God for the enormous part he – and the spirit-world generally – have played in creating us. We are God's 'children': he raised us.

Here then is theology's strange return: God did indeed create us in his own image, a truth that for us is now fully encapsulated or enclosed within a radical-humanist reading of the human condition. And I dare to assert that my academic colleagues who devote their lives to the critical-historical study of the origins and development of our great religions do actually hold my view, although they will furiously deny it. Of course they do, and of course they will. For modern critical theology itself (like modern Church history) has all along tacitly presupposed a radical-humanist vision of life, and therefore has been quietly preparing the ground for the new kind of religious thought that we are here to describe. Whether they like it or not, my worst enemies are, and cannot help but be, my secret allies.

The phrase 'Theology's Strange Return' also evokes another theme of this book, for the word 'return' reminds us of 'the return of the repressed' in psychoanalysis. In postmodernity Christianity is being progressively deconstructed, as text and subtext come apart and we begin to recognize that the religion was first created by a very large-scale act of repression. The original Jesus was far too radical a figure. He had to be very heavily veiled, and became the Christ of faith, the incarnate Word of God and the ever-obedient Son of his heavenly Father. Thus weirdly disguised, Jesus could be presented by apostles and priests as the central figure in a great myth of redemption which promises the believer a permanently *deferred* union with God that does *not* dethrone God. The object of the complicated manoeuvres here was to preserve just a little bit of what Jesus had been about while yet retaining in full the divine transcendence, the supernatural world, the system of religious mediation, and, above all, priestly and disciplinary power. But in postmodernity it is all coming apart. We begin to see that historical ecclesiastical Christianity was from the first constituted by a great repression of something bigger and better that lies behind it, something that is now at last coming into view.

The task of stripping away layer upon layer of pious falsification takes a long time, and encounters a good deal of resistance. For example, in the English-speaking world the liturgical year rises to a kind of popular peak with the singing in King's College Chapel of Mrs C. F. Alexander's hymn 'Once in royal David's city', describing the childhood of Jesus:

> And through all his wondrous childhood
> He would honour and obey ...
> Christian children all must be
> Mild, obedient, good as he.

William Blake, in 'The Everlasting Gospel', already protests against the falsity of this image of a 'creeping Jesus'. In the canonical Gospels there is only one childhood narrative, and it is a story of *dis*obedience:

> Was Jesus humble? Or did he
> Give any proofs of Humility? ...
> When but a child he ran away
> And left his parents in dismay.
> When they had wandered three days long
> These were the words upon his tongue:
> 'No earthly parents I confess:
> 'I am doing my Father's business.'

Today, every student learns that the Lucan story to which Blake appeals is *itself* also merely pious *midrash*, being based upon a similar story about the infant Samuel.

When, however, we acknowledge that virtually the *whole* of the received 'life of Christ' is little better than pious *midrash*, and confine ourselves strictly to the earliest and best-attested sayings-tradition; and then, more strictly still, confine ourselves to the simplest and most polished one-liners – then a very different picture begins to emerge. Not even Kierkegaard, nor even Nietzsche himself, grasped the full implications of a simple line in Q/Luke: 'Why don't you judge for yourselves what is right?'[7] Various very well-attested sayings elsewhere see good and evil, purity and impurity as springing from the human heart alone; for example: 'What goes into you can't defile you; what comes out of you can.'[8]

In effect, Jesus is a sharp critic of every kind of heteronomy, and one of the most important pioneers anywhere of thoroughgoing ethical autonomy (or 'subjectivism', or 'non-realism'). He liberates human beings from the old oppressive regime of 'Divine Law', natural moral law and the like. He is the Prometheus of morality, who brought ethical sovereignty and legislative power down from heaven and gave them to us. Nothing out there tells us how we must live: we and we alone can now with confidence knowingly trust our own hearts, and admit that we do and must invent our own ethics. Who else before Nietzsche said this so plainly, in the confidence that this was a profoundly liberating and empowering doctrine? So Jesus, even on my now thoroughly secular and post-Christian understanding of him, is still a great liberator of humankind.

Of course 'the knowledge of good and evil' is promised to humankind in the Hebrew Bible. So is the internalization of the moral law within the human heart, and the outpouring of the divine Spirit. A great deal of what I am here trying to say was already being said in Christian theological language. Law is succeeded by Grace, and by a new kind of moral freedom – and so on. But so long as it was believed as dogma, it couldn't be taken seriously, because 'belief', in the popular sense, is such a confused state of mind. Ecclesiastical Christianity was never seriously believed and perhaps never *could* be, for belief upon authority in a mystery you cannot understand is not clear belief. Only when we stop believing, and dismantle the old religious language, do we begin to see clearly just how clear and radically new Jesus' ethical message was. So new, that it could be assimilated and presented only in mythologized, pietized, mystified form. So it was, and is: the truth in ecclesiastical Christianity was buried so cleverly and so deeply that only with the death and dissolution of the old religion has it at last been able to come to light. 'I have said, "You are gods" ', is a biblical line; but only now can we begin to take it seriously.[9]

So I was trying to say in a book called *Jesus and Philosophy*. I sent out a pile of copies to theologians, but few noticed what I was talking about. And that is my third and last preliminary illustration of what I mean by 'Theology's Strange Return' *after* the death of God and the end of the dogmatic-ecclesiastical type of faith.

Next the question arises of what the following chapters yield. What does it all add up to, and what sort of new shape might religion assume in the future? Wait and see. Be warned that because some of the central ideas to be presented here are new and strange, I do need to be irritatingly repetitious at times.

D. C.
Cambridge, Christmas 2009

The Return of Eternity within Pure Transience

The first strange return to be considered is a very old one. Historically, eternity – often not clearly distinguished from everlasting duration, or 'sempiternity' – was attributed only to God, to the heavenly world, and to the kind of life there lived by the blessed. It was closely associated with immortality, perfection and incorruptibility, and was therefore very sharply contrasted with everything in the visible world here below. In the visible world everything was transient, merely contingent and changeable, and therefore corruptible, and ultimately mortal.

All this meant that the two worlds, the world of the immortal gods and the world of mortal men, were very sharply contrasted. The Greek immortal/mortal and eternity/time contrasts were in effect the same contrast as the ancient Hebrew contrast between 'spirit' and 'flesh'. Thus the prophet Isaiah encourages Israel not to be intimidated by Egypt: 'The Egyptians are men, and not God', he says: 'and their horses are flesh, and not spirit' (31.3). 'Flesh' is biological life; flesh is meat. It is transient, vulnerable and, above all, *mortal*. When it is said that in marriage man and woman become 'one flesh', we are to understand that this union of two mortals is death-haunted from its beginning, and throughout. 'All flesh is grass', says Isaiah (40.6) and a familiar Chinese proverb declares that men are 'straw dogs', death-fodder, made but to be burnt.

By contrast, spirit is everywhere supernatural, charged up with life and fizzing energy. It is sempiternal, in the sense that it lives on for ever. It may light upon, and even for a while indwell, a human being. But it is only a temporary resident: in Genesis, Yahweh explains: 'My spirit shall not abide in man for ever, for he is flesh . . .' (6.3).

The contrast between flesh and spirit is on the whole very clearly and consistently marked out and adhered to in the Bible, and it is a contrast between two distinct realms of being – the same contrast as the one that was already deeply embedded in Greek thought, and by Plato was built into the main tradition of Western philosophy. The popular contrast between 'Jewish thought' and 'Greek thought' is a mistake: rather, the two traditions are profoundly similar, so that for so long as Western philosophy has remained *au fond* Platonic, so long it has also remained profoundly religious. As Philo of Alexandra declared in antiquity, Plato was but Moses speaking Attic Greek. (Or, if you are really up to date, the authors of the Hebrew Bible rewrote Plato in Classical Hebrew.[10])

By the same token, just as in biblical thought the two worlds could briefly intersect, or even be conjoined, as when spirit manifested itself to a man who was but flesh, or even 'indwelt' a human being, so too in Greek thought the eternal might be manifested or briefly embodied in the human realm.

In classical Christianity the theme of the self-manifestation of eternal Being in the human world is taken very much further. In both the traditional and the contemporary senses of the word, Christ is 'iconic': he is the *eikōn* of the invisible God, the founding and definitive image of the Eternal One within human history. In him spirit and flesh were *permanently* conjoined: he was 'God from everlasting, man for evermore'. All the more calamitous, then, has been the total loss of the very idea of eternal Being and an eternal world during the past two centuries. The whole supernatural order has simply collapsed, leaving only the temporal flux of Becoming. It seems that the entire eternal world has disappeared without remainder.

Yet the interesting paradox is that during the last years of the eighteenth century, in the period of the turn to human subjectivity – the growth of 'the mind', psychology, feeling, history, Romanticism – in this period the notion of the eternal, instead of just vanishing, began to be deployed in fresh ways. Here I am thinking not only of people like Wordsworth,[11] who was raised in the old Christian-Platonic high culture and had some intimation of what was going on in philosophy, but also of people who did not have that education at all, but who still speak of eternity in the new way: people like Blake, J. M. W. Turner and John Clare. Take, for example, what Turner says about the meaning of the sun for him ('the sun is God') along with a familiar verse from Blake dated 1793, and a couplet from Clare:

> He who binds to himself a joy
> Doth the winged life destroy
> But he who kisses the joy as it flies
> Lives in Eternity's sun rise.[12]

> I snatched the sun's eternal ray
> And wrote till earth was but a name.[13]

The question is, How can the notion of eternity still have application in a world in which everything is transient? The sun is only a fire. It burns, and in due course will burn out and die, as all stars do. What does the new notion of eternity amount to?

Blake and Turner associate eternity very strongly with the sun, which is the single grandest image of heedless, self-expending, glorious generosity. It pours out, and it passes away. We should live like that, loving all that is transient without clutching at it, unreservedly identifying ourselves with the 'brightness' of the pouring out and passing away of all things.

Why is this a regaining of 'eternity'? Oddly enough, it is a secularization of one strand in the traditional idea of God. There was always a difficulty in imagining how a fully Platonic and timeless God could be in some sense personal.

The best answer orthodox theism could give was to say that God is 'pure act', always at full stretch, always fully expressing himself, changelessly *all out*; and secondly, that the time of God's life is a *nunc stans*, a standing Now that embraces everything. And so it is with us: we should forget all our reservations and anxieties, and give ourselves wholly to the present fleeting moment, the 'Nu', as Eckhart calls it. We should be empty of clutching, empty of self, empty of all the old ideas of *substance*. We should be 'lost in the objectivity of world-love', as I have elsewhere put it; or, perhaps better, we should let ourselves be only an empty space filled with brightness. Life lived like that is 'eternal' life.

The word brightness (in Heidegger, *Lichtung*) is important. It goes back to the Greek verb *phainō*, *phainomai*, meaning to shine, to show, to manifest.[14] It is the word traditionally used in connection with a god's self-revelation, as in *epiphany* and *theophany*, but it is also the word used for the flux of sense-experiences, *phenomena*. 'Phenomena' are streaming bright appearances or seemings, and it was perhaps Claude Monet who was the first major artist successfully to make mere phenomena the subject of his art. In his very best work he paints water, leaves, shadows and dancing sunlight, and shows us how there can be a return of Eternity in the very midst of pure transience. In some ways, the insight here is ancient. There are familiar examples in a number of mystical writers, both Christian and East Asian Buddhist. But Monet has very successfully *democratized* or laicized the experience of eternal happiness found in the midst of everyday visual experience, and that is not a little thing.

Finally, notice that it is because the sun is everywhere such a powerful image of God, and because everyone understands the illumination of the entire visible world by sunlight, that the sun has since the late eighteenth century been the obvious bridge between the old theological idea of eternity and the new experiential notion of eternity. So it is that eternal life of the old, lost kind has returned to us as solar living.

And another curiosity: I am suggesting that we can and do regain eternity when we are so immersed in life, in moral action, or in aesthetic contemplation, that we completely forget about time and anxiety. Did that remind you of Kant's doctrine that moral action is timeless?

2

The Return of the Creative Power of Language

Around five thousand years ago the Egyptian First Dynasty united Upper and Lower Egypt, establishing its capital at Memphis, where the 'Two Lands' met. This in effect made Ptah, the god of Memphis, into the supreme God and indeed the universal Creator, and gave his priests at Memphis a great theological opportunity. They needed to tell a very grand creation-story; but what was the best imagery for the creative action and the self-expression of One Mighty God? Other temples – Heliopolis, Hermopolis – told stories about how Atum or Re had created the other gods and the world by masturbation, by spitting, by sneezing, or by vomiting, but the priests at Memphis were evidently intellectual types who wanted a loftier kind of production than that. For them the grandest and best image of divine power going out into creative expression was our human production and employment of *language*. It is by this power that we ourselves are able to become unified selves and productive agents; and at the divine level it is by the same power of thought and utterance that Ptah has created and ordered the entire world of gods and men. The Memphite priests seem clear about the analogy they are developing, and indeed the Shabaka stone on which the Memphite theology is preserved, is one of the very best surviving examples of 'philosophy before philosophy'.[15]

From Memphis to Nietzsche, through five thousand years of writing, it is easy to trace the idea that *Dichtung*, 'strong' poetry, commanding and creative utterance, is the most powerful force we know of. For example, in Hebrew the 'Ten Commandments', as we call them, are just the Ten 'Words': the imperative, commanding use of language is assumed to be primary because all utterance is an expression of *power*. Or again, Neoplatonic philosophers and early Christian theologians exactly repeated the thinking of the Memphite theologians when they distinguished between the *Logos endiathētos* and the *Logos prophorikos*, the Word latent in the Divine Mind and the Word 'proceeding' or coming out into creative expression. And again, in the great days of monarchy and right up to Early Modern times, it was obvious to all that a human king's rule was mediated by creative linguistic actions. He signed into law, he authorized, he dubbed, he created: his word had to be obeyed and his 'writ' must run throughout his realm. How did it ever come about that, for a while at least, we lost the idea of the *speech-act*, the idea that every authoritative utterance is a *deed* that changes things?

What disturbed our understanding of the nature of language for two or three centuries was the rise of modern natural science. Bishop Thomas Sprat, writing his *History of the Royal Society* (1667),[16] describes how the early members of the Society set about their task of collecting, reviewing and publishing fresh additions to the received body of scientific knowledge. Scientific reports addressed to the society must be couched in the very plainest and clearest descriptive language, using precisely defined and univocal technical terms. There must be no flamboyant rhetoric, and no expressions of personal feeling: nothing personal at all, in fact, because science sets out to see the world from the viewpoint of an ideal finite observer who may be anyone. Any competent observer, looking at the same thing and familiar with the same standard terminology, would see the same thing and say the same things about it.

Science, we gather, involves a rigorously impersonal and standardized kind of descriptive language, and within a generation the extraordinary triumph of Newton's *Principia* persuaded people that they had a new way of knowledge, the most potent that human beings have ever devised. Not surprisingly, many concluded that the best way to truth and the most powerful sort of language is one that is the most rigorously impersonal, objective and purely descriptive. A true sentence is a kind of diagram that seeks as accurately as possible to copy an independently existing extra-linguistic fact. Language from henceforth must be seen as coming *second*. It doesn't shape reality: it *copies* reality. You should aim at a clear one-to-one match between each word in the sentence and the corresponding feature of the state of affairs it reports.

That is English 'literalism'. As late as 1912 Russell and the young Wittgenstein were still trying to make it work by spelling out the logic of it really exactly. (They failed.) Later, George Orwell was a writer still enthralled by it; and even to-day people still invoke the old theory by the way they use the adjective 'literally'. As when someone exclaims: 'I am *literally* speechless!' (Don't take that too literally.)

It should be acknowledged that the rise of science is not the only source of English literalism. In the controversies of the Reformation the authorities often demanded subscription to creeds and confessional statements taken 'in the literal and grammatical sense'.[17] In addition, many Protestant Reformers like Calvin claimed that ordinary men could read Scripture for themselves, taking it in its 'literal' sense, and could find salvation in it unaided – an idea that still influences modern Evangelicals, who take, as it is said, a 'literalistic' view of the Bible. So there was a religious kind of literalism even before the rise of modern science. It arose in connection with the struggle for religious democratization at the end of the Middle Ages, and is even echoed in the French phrase *au pied de la lettre*.

However, English literalism was particularly encouraged by the stupendous success of the new 'experimental philosophy', and there can be no doubt that it has gradually eroded people's ability to understand religious action and expression. Religion is of its nature very highly self-involving:

inevitably, it suffers when people come to equate truth with impersonal detachment and objectivity. Inevitably, it comes to be thought that the more rigorously truthful you become, the further you will move away from religion. Religiousness comes to be viewed as a 'bias' that causes one to swerve away from objectivity.

Today there is no reason why we should any longer be led astray by literalistic ideas about the relation of language to reality. Instead of supposing that we first see an ordered, intelligible world of fact all about us, and *then* set out to describe it in fact-copying sentences, we have come to realize that (as Gilles Deleuze has put it) it is *we* who give the orders. It is something like programming in our heads that converts the fast-changing and disorderly chaos of raw experience into knowledge of an ordered, stable external world. Objectivity isn't given to us in and with our experience: we give objectivity *to* our experience by the framework into which we fit it. Kant gave the classical analysis of what this programming must consist of, namely, an apparatus of *concepts*. Later writers, more conscious than he of the historical and cross-cultural diversity of all world-views, redescribed the programming as *culture*. Later still, it was redescribed again as *language*. Gradually we have come to understand that the bright, beautiful, ordered world that we see, and are ourselves parts of, is our own construct. It is no longer seen as having been created once and for all by the commanding language of God, but as being continuously made, renegotiated and remade within our own human conversation. We create the world, and the laws of nature are not discovered but invented. You won't find Newton's laws out there. They don't exist out there: you'll find them in a copy of his book *The Mathematical Principles of Natural Philosophy* (1687). Look at the world in this way, he says, work on these assumptions, and you'll find that a great many sums come out right, predictions are fulfilled and much is made clear. And so it turned out, and even today much of what Newton says still works well in most circumstances, even though (for very good reasons) his ideas are by now encapsulated within an enormously larger and more complex body of theory of which he himself knew nothing. Something similar has happened in the case of Darwin. He did not make a *discovery*: he recommended a certain way of looking at animals and plants which has proved so illuminating and fruitful that almost all of modern biology has been built around it. He was acutely aware of objections and difficulties with his theory to which he had no adequate reply. Since his time new theories about heredity, about the mathematics of natural selection, about cell biology and biochemistry, about the past movement of tectonic plates on the earth's crust, and about the ways in which the elementary constituents of organic life may have been scattered around the early universe – all this has hugely enlarged the story as originally told by Darwin. But it remains the case that science is a growing and developing *human* cultural activity. It is a very disciplined communal activity. It builds a public and therefore an *objective* world, the world we see and inhabit and deal with, *our* world. Since we have no knowledge of any world *not* formed by our theories and clothed in our language, and no knowledge of any absolute and suprahuman perspective upon the world to which we can appeal, our world as currently theorized by us is effectively *the* world. Of course it is. I'm perfectly happy to smile sweetly and agree with the most obdurate scientific realist, provided it be recognized that it is the strict *linguistic* discipline imposed upon scientists by the Royal Society, and all the other great learned societies, that makes scientific knowledge objective in the way it is. It was after all *we* who first invented 'objective reality' – in the person of René Descartes, in fact – and *we* who found in natural science the most powerful way yet of projecting it out.

And if our obdurate realist still objects, we must ask about where realism gets its ideas of reality and objectivity from? Our sensory nerves deliver to the brain nothing but an irregular crackle of different sorts of white noise. How on earth does the realist suppose that such a crackle can deliver to us our ideas about space and time, and indeed about mind-independent Reality, allegedly existing out there? After that, if the realist remains unconvinced we should ask for his or her remaining objections to be stated, please, in some medium other than human language. In return, we can promise the realist that we will surrender when he or she produces a martian or titanian textbook of physics containing physical theory *structurally* isomorphous with our own (though personally I'm sure that if titanian physicists are like enough to us to produce language, and in it physics that is structurally like ours, then *they'll* be bright enough to be non-realists too, my arguments being equally valid for them).

So much for the way in which the idea of the world-building power of language, so prominent not only in Genesis but throughout the Bible, has returned in postmodernity. The use of this power was originally restricted to God and to some few human beings such as prophets through whom God's spirit spoke his word. But in the course of the modern changeover from heterologous to autologous thinking, what we originally thought of as a divine power has been returned to us – or more exactly, has returned into language itself, the language in which we construct and reconstruct ourselves and our worlds.

People glimpsing this extraordinary truth feel it and write of it in different ways. Oscar Wilde says somewhere: 'Between me and reality there hangs always a mist of words.' Lucky him. My experience has been harder: it has been an experience of being made and unmade by language, repeatedly.

3

The Return of Grand Narrative as Archaeology of the Present

The roots of the idea of a Grand Narrative, as an all-inclusive and fully cosmic Story of Everything, run down deep into the past. The traditional Christian creeds have an approximately historical shape in that they run from Creation to the Last Judgement, and this form was not new. The Hebrew Bible contains many indications that the worship of ancient Israel commonly included a recitation of the mighty acts of God in the past through which the nation had first been brought into being, and since then had been delivered from various threats.[18] Ancient Roman rhetoric similarly required a major public speech to include a recitation of the various great deeds done in the past on behalf of the Republic.

Early Christianity quickly began to develop its own *Grand Récit*, as the French call it. St Paul laid the foundations,[19] as he thought about the history and the fate of the Jewish people and about the relation of the First to the Second Adam, and as he worked up the eschatology taught by John, Jesus and the earliest church into a general account of the final salvation of humankind as a whole. Next, Irenaeus (*c*. 130– *c*. 200) developed a little further the Latin understanding of Christ as 'recapitulating' all humanity in himself: and then the Latin Grand Narrative reached its fullest development in *The City of God* (written around 413–426) by Augustine of Hippo (354–430).

Augustine's version of the great Latin Christian Grand Narrative remained dominant in the culture until the late seventeenth century. John Calvin in particular stuck so close to Augustine and was so Grand-Narrative-minded that preachers in his tradition (variously called Reformed, Calvinist, Presbyterian or puritan) long tended to maintain that the entire story, the Plan of Salvation, was implicit in every verse of Scripture and should therefore emerge and be retold in every sermon. The great story gave meaning to the ordinary believer's life by promising him or her a small but preassigned and definite place in a sweeping epic of universal redemption. Final blessedness was assured: if you had ever tasted divine grace, then you could be certain of your own part in the victory celebrations. This was called Final Perseverance.

Despite his less than fully orthodox theology, John Milton still believed the old story (*Paradise Lost*, 1667; *Paradise Regained*, 1671). But within a generation Newton's work made it certain that Western culture had changed over, and had changed permanently, to a *secular* cosmology based on mathematical physics. In the same way the old theological kind of historical writing gave way to the new document-based and continuous secular-narrative kind of history, if not with Clarendon's *History of the Rebellion* (1688), then certainly in the work of writers like Hume and Gibbon. For a while it could still continue to be claimed that Genesis was the best available source for human origins and human history up to the very beginning of the Iron Age, and Middle-Eastern archaeology was directed towards confirming the biblical narrative. But slowly and in many cases very reluctantly, 'biblical archaeology' was given up as a wild-goose chase. Today, fully secularized cosmology and history have expanded so much that it is now hard for any of us to imagine what it must have been like to be a person like John Bunyan, a high-class figure of excellent ability, but completely enclosed within the horizon of a religious Grand-Narrative vision of the world. Compared with Bunyan, even the most provincial and blinkered Bible-belt creationist of today has already been at least three-quarters secularized by access to modern medicine, modern weather forecasting and modern electronic communications technologies.

The old Grand-Narrative sacred cosmology has, then, been clearly on the way out since the late 1680s; but many people have clung on to it, or to bits of it, for as long as possible, and two secular and political updatings of it remained popular until well within living memory. Both were historicist and very optimistic: one was the old Enlightenment radical belief in 'the perfectibility of Man',[20] and the other was Marxism. The last relics of 'literal' belief in both of them melted away between the 1960s and the 1980s, leaving our own generation finally orphaned, without any comforting Grand-Narrative ideology at all. For most people today life has become a matter of routine, boredom and the steady drift towards personal extinction. We still want our children to know about the world we have lost, and the most popular children's writers still purvey Grand-Narrative-pastiche epics.[21] Popular art and entertainment, and especially spectator sports, may offer welcome distraction to ordinary people, but the underlying mood of 'calm despair' or 'settled melancholy' has by now been fixed for a long time – perhaps ever since these phrases were coined in the nineteenth century by Tennyson and Hardy. More recently, Claude Lévi-Strauss (d. 2009) used the phrase 'serene pessimism'.

How can we cope with this modern condition, which in postmodernity appears quite inescapable? There is no likelihood at all of our being able to rediscover some great necessitating power outside ourselves – God, or History, for example – that will sweep us up into its own triumphant march onwards and upwards. Not a hope: our life is and will from now on remain outsideless. But there is a much better possibility, if we learn how to pursue what Michel Foucault called 'the archaeology of the present'. The fundamental problem of life today is our need to understand and accept what we have become, and how we got here. In every faculty of the modern university, and certainly in every faculty which is at all historically minded, this question is the elephant in the room, huge, maybe unseen and maybe not often referred to, but always *there*. Only ten or fifteen generations ago we still lived within the horizon of a great religion-based sacred civilization. Then came the avalanche: in rapid succession, the Renaissance, Early Modernity, Enlightenment, the democratic revolutions, and the roaring development of science-based industrial civilization, until finally we hit postmodernity, and have found ourselves in an empty glaring culture with no future for the individual, and a very dark prospect confronting the race.

What sense can we hope to make of this extraordinary history? There's a temptation to try to reinstate the old kind of Grand Narrative by asking: 'Where did we all go wrong?' That would be a mistake, because the 350-year story of progressive disenchantment or disillusionment that we have collectively gone through is irreversible. There is no way back: 'You can't go home again,' as the memorable novel title has it.[22] The critical type of thinking, applied to every area of our ideal culture, has progressively uprooted all our former deep assumptions – *including* the assumption that the whole of cosmic history has been created as a great epic narrative with a beginning, a middle and an end, a narrative that gives meaning, value and an aim to your life and to mine, and is actually recorded for us in our Holy Book.[23] Actually, our assumptions have been so comprehensively exposed and uprooted that we have lost all the old 'absolutes' or fixed points, including even our ideas of any objective 'reality' independent of what is built into the background of our current conversation. Reality? – today it's like walking through the night market in a great East Asian city. A thrilling dance of signs in the dark. And that's all there is, and there's no way back: no possibility of restoring the type of world-view that we have finally and irretrievably lost. Once we have consciously lost the old, deep unconscious assumptions, we cannot consciously readopt them and become unconscious of them again.

However, there does still remain one creative possibility. Just as each of us needs to try to tell the story of her or his own life, so collectively we do need to keep on telling, debating and retelling the story of how we have become the people we now find ourselves to be, and why in order to become ourselves we have had to follow such a circuitous route. In this endeavour to make sense of ourselves and of our human situation as we now perceive it, by telling stories about how we got here and why we had to come this way – in this great communal endeavour we are trying to produce our own new kind of Grand Narrative.

The story has to explain why we had to take such a long diversion through *metaphysics* (Parmenides to Nietzsche – twenty-four centuries?), or through *belief in God* (full realistic monotheism, Philo to Hume – about seventeen centuries?), or through *belief in spirits and other mythic beings* (some tens of millennia?). But we need to be able to tell the story in such a way that we may look back with gratitude and affection, and not only with painful regret and nostalgia, at our spiritual past and also can cheerfully say Yes to the kind of empty selfhood and transient life that is available to us now.

Elsewhere I have two or three times tried to outline the form such a new Grand Narrative might take.[24] When language first began to move it gave us the beginnings of mind and selfhood, by opening up to us a huge flood of alternative possibilities, regrets and threats. Because words are general, they don't just form and fix the state of affairs presently before us: they also hint at and bring to mind a vast range of other possible states of affairs, creating a kind of mental overload. But because early man was already a keyed-up, anxious animal, all this extra anxiety was too much to handle. People felt disabled and terrified. We needed to find some sort of picture of ourselves and our situation-in-life, but these topics were simply not yet thinkable directly or 'autologously'. We could only begin to construct a picture-to-work-by of ourselves and our life by learning to think 'heterologously'. We thought of beings unlike ourselves who *did* understand themselves and were quite sure of their own power and mobility. These beings did control nature, did know what to do, and so on, and it was by thinking about them, and of ourselves as their servants, that we humans gradually grew in the confidence that one day we'd be able to unify, understand and control ourselves, our society and our world. When that day came we would be able to say goodbye to heterologous thinking and ethical heteronomy, for we would be ready to be autologous thinkers and autonomous agents. Thus the supernatural order (and for that matter, metaphysical philosophy too) played an essential role in the education of the human race. And that explains why theology really was the queen of the sciences for so long. For it was only *via* the idea of God that we were able to develop all our ideas about a unified self, reason, a unified law-governed cosmos, sovereignty, property, supervision (Providence) and management, long-term purposes and action to attain them and so on. God taught us everything, so that we are eternally grateful to God even as we now leave him behind.

Remember, though, that this Just-So story is not a real, objectively true Grand Narrative. It's a story I made up because I needed to bridge the gap between a quivering, highly strung animal and ourselves. How on earth did we get from there to here? The old mythico-religious world-view was a complex, protective, educational fiction which was as true as anything can be for as long as we really believed it, and it worked for us, it helped to make us what we have become. I'm happy to love it and leave it, while still carrying along with me something – indeed, rather a lot – of what it has taught me. Thus the old Augustinian Grand Narrative of Creation, Fall and Redemption has come back to me, retold as the story of the path our forebears had to take in order to get to where we all are now.

4

The Return of God as Life

Philosophy in the main Western tradition was normally concerned only with 'pure reason' – that is, with Plato's ideal world of timeless intelligible truths: truths mathematical, logical and metaphysical. Only gradually was it persuaded to come down to earth and address itself to human bodily life in time. Early Modern discussions of life usually followed Aristotle and Plato in focusing on *biological*, rather than cultural, life. Life was the power of growth and movement. It was seen in terms of blood and warmth. The soul was the principle of life . . . and so on. Thus far hardly any advance had been made on pre-philosophical religious thought.

When Kant in his later years came to write about art, he found himself (rather reluctantly) compelled to take up the subjects of life, desire, feeling, pleasure, and even the body. His basic doctrine runs something like this: life is the capacity to picture something, desire it, make a move for it, and feel pleasure in attaining it. When I attain something that I have desired, not only do I feel immediate pleasure, but also I enjoy an internal promotion or enhancement of my own life-feeling; and here Kant is evidently speaking for the first time of what we would now call *jouissance*, *joie de vivre* or 'the joys of life'.[25]

As Kant (who is clearly uneasy about the whole subject) finds himself opening up modern human philosophy – philosophy of life and of the body – he begins to link himself with the Romantic Movement, then getting under way.[26] One sees why the *Critique of Judgement* (1790), and in particular his philosophy of art, was the part of Kant's work that appealed most to his young contemporaries. Against the whole dominant tradition in the West, he is admitting that our aesthetic response to architecture and sculpture, and even to music, is a matter of bodily feeling. To enjoy art, it's no good being a pure spirit; you have to be a living, embodied human be-ing in time. Good art, as they say, *turns you on*: that's how it works, and it was foolish ever to have pretended otherwise.

So Kant's philosophy of art became part of a massive cultural turn away from the eternal world and towards the world of history, from God to Man, from idealized Reason to the emotions, and from things changeless to things transient: a cultural turn whose consequences are still being worked out.

One of the first and most obvious effects of the shift was the Death of God. In the years 1799–1800 came the great 'Atheism Controversy' around the views of Kant's follower, J. G. Fichte. Since Fichte, no major philosopher has successfully revived the old metaphysical theism; but two great figures, namely Hegel and Kierkegaard, made ingenious attempts to conceal or defer the Death of God while yet accepting the new romantic moves, whether towards historical development through a dialectic of forces, or towards passionate, struggling, individual human subjectivity. Both men attempted to solve the great problem of the age: how could faith in God in any form survive, in a restless, purely human world that appeared completely to exclude God? For Hegel, history was God's own *Bildungsroman*; for Kierkegaard, if we couldn't cognize the Absolute, we could at least touch it in the darkness by the absolute passion of our own faith commitment to it.

A third figure of the early nineteenth century, Ludwig Feuerbach, had another answer to this last question: in standard Christian dogmatic teaching, he pointed out, God has become Man. The incarnation of God in man, as man, is supposed to be plenary and permanent. In Christ, the Eternal Son is 'God from everlasting, man for evermore'. Furthermore, the humanity with which God has fully and permanently united himself is not merely that of one human individual:

it is generic humanity, and even (some would say) the concrete universal humanity of the whole human race. And it is also standard Christian doctrine that henceforth Jesus Christ is the only way to God: God cannot be known except via the universal human which his Son has taken to himself. But if all this is true, then the current turn in Western thought from metaphysical theism to radical (and *social*) humanism is merely the historical completion of a turn that was implicit in Christianity almost from the very first.[27]

Feuerbach's argument here was anticipated by William Blake:

> Thou art a Man; God is no more,
> [i.e., 'no more than human']
> Thy own Humanity learn to adore,
> For that is my Spirit of life . . . [28]

The classic radical-theology argument that Blake here states so concisely comes straight out of mainline Protestantism. Emphasizing human fallenness, the great Reformers were sceptical about the power of natural, unaided human reason. They disparaged metaphysics, rational theology, and natural human religiosity, declaring that there is no way to God except through Jesus Christ and his saving work. But if in Christ there is a definite, complete and final incarnation of God in generic humanity, and if there is no other way to salvation *except* through Christ, then the saving death of Christ on the cross is also the Death of God, and only the slightest nudge is needed in order to tip the highest Protestant orthodoxy over into pure atheistic religious humanism. Which indeed was done by the leading German thinkers between Kant and Marx, between the 1780s and the 1840s. The Protestant Reformers said that the man Jesus Christ is all there is of God for us, and Marx said that Man is the highest being for man. So where's the difference? Only that God has been brought down into our human-life-time, and thrown forward to become a mighty developing process, the evolving human life-world that Hegel calls *Geist* and Marx calls History; and the whole vast process of rewriting God as Culture, as the developing mental life of all humankind, is seen as revealing the inner meaning of Christianity in general, and of the incarnation of God in man in particular. So influential has this story been that even the great exponent of Calvinist neo-orthodoxy, Karl Barth himself, could end his career by writing about the with-man-ness, *Mittmenschlichkeit*, of God.

I have written a good deal – and no doubt too much – about the return of God as 'life' during the past decade or so.[29] God comes down into immanence; God is now the endless, all-inclusive world of human striving and human symbolic exchange that has produced us and within which we live and move and have our being. And so we begin to see the modern secular-humanist West as the perfectly legitimate heir and continuator of the Christian tradition.[30]

The new sense of 'life' sees it as being chiefly human historical and cultural life. It is 'the fray' that we love so much, a mixture of political struggle and communicative exchange, like marriage. But a little of the older, predominantly biological, notion of life lingers yet, and remains important to us when we think of life as being unstoppably, endlessly, automobile, self-affirming, self-outpouring, self-renewing – and also in many ways rather *dense* and mysterious in its texture. In the older Western tradition there was one, just one, writer who grasped this and wrote really well about it, namely Meister Eckhart. In this I suspect Eckhart was influenced by the Hebrew Bible, which does not make such a clear natural/supernatural distinction as later orthodoxies usually did. On the contrary, ancient Jewish thought tended to blur together Spirit, breath and wind, and it similarly tended to blur together the life of God and the power of life in semen, in the genitals, and in natural fertility generally. Certainly Eckhart talks as if he is ready simply to equate God with the outpouring energy of life in ourselves: 'God's being is my life.'[31]

5

The Return of God as Brightness

I saw Eternity the other night
Like a great *Ring* of pure and endless light,
All calm, as it was bright,
And round beneath it, Time in hours, days, years,
Driv'n by the spheres
Like a vast shadow mov'd . . .[32]

Following a tradition that goes back to Plato, Henry Vaughan
(1621/2–1695) describes the Eternal World in terms of a circle
or sphere, and as brilliant light. In the eternal world, everything is perfectly intelligible, luminously clear and explicit.
There is no duplicity: nothing is shadowy or veiled. God,
being pure actuality, is always all-out like the sun which, in
the Bible as everywhere else, is always the chief image of the
Divine.

In a poem called 'The Retreate', Vaughan takes up the theme
of Wordsworth's Immortality Ode. The soul pre-existed in the
Eternal World, which is why a little angel-brightness clings
still to the human infant, and why the child's perception of
the world is still irradiated with something of the brightness
of heaven:

Happy those early dayes! When I
Shin'd in my Angell-infancy.
Before I understood this place
Appointed for my second race,
Or taught my soul to fancy ought (*sic*: aught)
But a white Celestial thought,

When yet I had not walked above
A mile, or two, from my first love,
And looking back (at that short space,)
Could see a glimpse of his bright-face;
When on some *gilded Cloud* or *flowre*
My gazing soul would dwell an houre,
And in those weaker glories spy
Some shadows of eternity . . .[33]

The analogy is natural, and runs very close: as the rays of the sun may gild a cloud or make vegetation glow with luminosity, so earthly things in general may reflect a little of the intense light that surrounds their Creator. Note that created things are certainly not yet perceived as being bright on their own account: their brightness is secondary and reflected, like the brightness of the moon, in which

Wise Nicodemus saw such light
As made him know his God by night.[34]

In this latter poem, 'The Night', Vaughan considers the nature of the divine light. In the Bible, God is described both as unapproachably brilliant light *and* as deep darkness. How can that be? It was customary to answer by pointing to the sun, whose light is so bright that we cannot gaze at it directly. Eagles can do so, it was believed, and the Fourth Evangelist was symbolically an eagle; but we? – for us, God's light is blinding. And here writers might distinguish between the intellectual light of perfectly clear understanding, and the more nearly 'material' light of the eyes.

All this could soon become tiresome, but Vaughan next produces a memorable phrase, which he may have lifted from one of the mystics:

There is in God (some say)
A deep but dazling darkness . . .[35]

Vaughan's devotional poetry was the work of a devout Anglican in exile during the 1650s. It is a confident expression of the leading doctrines of Christian Platonism, and is unwaveringly theocentric. As such, it makes an excellent foil or sounding board against which to test the Immortality Ode of Wordsworth, published just 150 years later.[36]

At first sight, little has changed. Wordsworth seems to be talking just the same language as Vaughan, and using it to express the same nostalgia for lost glories: nostalgia for childhood and nostalgia for the eternal world, bound up together. But on closer examination we begin to see a great difference between the two poets.

In the first place, Wordsworth is nothing like so clearly and consistently theocentric in outlook as Vaughan. Vaughan is orthodox: for him brightness is glory, and it always belongs primarily to God, and only secondarily is transferred to and reflected by God's creatures. But Wordsworth is not orthodox. He lives in a time when human subjectivity is being affirmed, and the real subject of his poetry is always himself, and especially the growth and development of his own mind. In the *Fenwick Notes* Wordsworth commented that the Immortality Ode had its origin in his childhood sense of 'the indomitableness of the spirit within me'.[37] This means that in an age of critical thinking, with the end of metaphysical realism, a whole lot of things that used to be seen as existing objectively are coming to be *internalized*, as in the popular phrase about 'beauty being in the eye of the beholder'. In the *Fenwick Notes* Wordsworth freely acknowledges that for him the pre-existence of the human soul in the heavenly world was a fiction, a popular and Platonic belief. He's a non-realist, but quite happy to make use of fictions when he needs them: 'I took hold of the notion of pre-existence as having sufficient foundation in humanity for authorizing me to make the best use of it I could as a poet.'[38] Notice too that Wordsworth departs from the classical tradition in wanting to emphasize and to explore the profound changes of consciousness that we undergo as we pass through the successive stages of a long life. He doesn't hold the old view of the soul as a finite spiritual substance that cannot disintegrate and therefore is immortal and even in some sense unchanging. He is a non-realist about the soul, but he persists in the feeling that 'some part of our nature is imperishable'.[39]

In the context of all this the 'brightness' or 'glory' whose loss the Immortality Ode laments so unforgettably is clearly subjective. When we were very young everything was fresh and new. The doors of perception were clean, and that first freshness cannot ever be recovered. Or so Wordsworth thought. Today we know otherwise. If under local anaesthetic and with the latest technology you have a cataract removed and a new clear lens slipped into an eye, then you can to a breathtaking degree regain the full glory of childhood perception of the world for the next few days. Much the same heightened quivering brilliance and super-reality of the visual world is reported by various people in connection with extravertive mysticism, with some hallucinogenic drugs such as those tried out by Aldous Huxley, with Post-Impressionist and Fauve painting, and (in some people) with the onset of an epileptic fit. I have known the first and third of those four.

Thus brightness is a matter of the way we see the world, and not of the way things are objectively – and Wordsworth was of course well aware that objectivity is not purely given, but arises from the way the mind and the world interact. As he puts it in 'Home at Grasmere':

How exquisitely the individual Mind
(And the progressive powers perhaps no less
Of the whole species) to the external world
Is fitted; and how exquisitely too . . .
the external world is fitted to the mind;
And the creation (by no lower name
Can it be called) which they with blended might
Accomplish: this is my great argument.[40]

Wordsworth was certainly wordy: he knew ten European languages. But he did not know German, and was dependent upon the very unreliable Coleridge for his slight and hazy knowledge of the great things that were going on in German philosophy at that time. Nevertheless, he is clearly highly aware of the great changeover from the old God-centred, metaphysical world-view to a new outlook based on critical thinking and on starting from the finite human subject. That means, thinking *autologously* – thinking as what one is, and from where one is.

And what of brightness? The old Christian-Platonist and theological kind of brightness was very eloquently described by various religious poets and writers of the seventeenth century. After Vaughan, Thomas Traherne is perhaps the best of them. In the theory of art, Ruskin clung to something like Christian Platonism right up to the moment in the 1850s when he lost his faith. But in Wordsworth it is already clear that the experience of and wonder at brightness is becoming detached from God and secularized. It needs a new rationale: what is brightness now?

By talking of brightness I have in mind roughly what George Berkeley meant by speaking of 'a divine visual language'. Of several of our senses, but of the sense of sight most of all, it has to be said that a sense-experience is not just a mere stimulus. It is highly conscious – in fact, it is *lit up* with consciousness. We don't just see: we *see* that we see, and we always see a complete and shining world with no gaps or edges, a world in which we are aware of being ourselves situated.

In parenthesis, I believe there are people to whom the sense of hearing gives a complete world, and a very rich world. Among other mammals, there are some (for example, dogs) whose sense of smell is very rich and informative, and others (for example, some small rodents) whose whiskers alone keep half their grey matter busy. But I know nothing of these latter, because like most people I am very visual. All my life, I've been led chiefly by my eyesight. But what makes our human vision so very bright? Most other mammals, and certainly nearly all herbivores, have only the limited, specialized kind of vision their way of life requires for survival – seeing their food, detecting the approach of a predator, and so on. But why the truly remarkable brightness of human vision?

Heidegger hints at the answer. We see a language-formed world, in which our own language has already formed, identified and theorized everything. We can name everything we see, we see in sentences what is going on, we have a scientific theory about everything we see, and we can read the history of everything we see; and all this is what Heidegger calls *Lichtung*, the lighting-up of the world by language. We see a world that has been made bright and beautiful by the way our language has differentiated, fixed, and attached a large body of theory to everything.

To put it in a single, dense sentence: our visual experience is very full and highly conscious because we can in such detail *tell* what we are looking at. Our visual world is hugely brightened by language. An analogy: get out your atlas and look at the map of Italy. Just how much of what's printed on the map accurately replicates stuff out there that you would see if you were to look down from a spaceship? Answer: only the coastline. Almost everything else on the map is a conventional sign, and not a copy of what may be seen from high up in the sky. Knowing how to read the map involves knowing how to use the map to generate a huge number of sentences about Italy and how to find your way around it. The analogy suggests how it is that by covering the world all over with signs we make it rich, interesting and bright. Indeed, just writing this paragraph has made me wish to visit Italy again.

In the Middle Ages, and indeed right up to the seventeenth century, people's knowledge of the world about them was astonishingly poor. Shakespeare knows his wild flowers, because of their symbolic and medicinal importance. But his theory and his ability to differentiate clouds, beetles and rocks; his ability to date and read the history of buildings and landscapes; his physics and chemistry, his history of art – all these were very poor indeed by our standards. He couldn't name a single butterfly. They were not named yet. The sun, the seasons, human faces and costumes, the weather and wild flowers – all these were bright for him, but that's about all. But before he died, people were just beginning to make the first effective use of telescopes and microscopes.

Brightness – the brightness of the visual world about us that so *fills our thoughts* (our visual field is also the field of our consciousness), this marvellous brightness has been created by our evolving language, our richer and richer descriptions. It is *glory*: a secular return of what used to be called the manifestation of the divine glory in the world of creation. And for me, the glory of God has returned in the glory of the visual field, and the light of language.

6

The Return of God as our Maker

For almost the whole history of the human species, we have been able to relate ourselves to life only via, and with the help of, an imaginary supernatural world of 'mythic beings', ancestors, spirits, angels, gods, the One God, and other unseen forces and agencies. There have been periods in late classical antiquity, in the early Italian Renaissance, and since the West European Enlightenment, when some people have done without any such belief, but only in very recent years has there been mass abandonment of religious belief. In England, people are still sometimes heard to say: 'Well, God made me that way', or 'After all, we are all children of God', as if to indicate that supernatural beliefs still play an important part in our popular philosophy of life; but today most people are quite secular for most of the time, and this prompts the question of why the supernatural world was so very important to so many people for so long.

Unbelievers have traditionally offered two main kinds of explanation. Belief in spirit-beings, says Thomas Hobbes,[41] is prompted by fear, superstition and ignorance as to the true causes of things; furthermore, religion is an almost uniquely powerful, non-rational and potentially dangerous political force, and it is very important that the leaders of society shall know how to manage and control it successfully. The best way to do this is to establish a very moderate form of religion that is unlikely to do much harm – the English solution. Hobbes was indeed himself an Anglican.

In a less provocative vein, Victorian anthropologists usually regarded tribal religious belief systems as primitive and proto-scientific hypotheses about the world.[42] When modern Western education reaches such people, their traditional beliefs will naturally fade away and be replaced by better, and tested, theories about the weather, about disease, about the heavenly bodies and so on. On this view, religion can disappear without leaving any sense of loss.

Wittgenstein had a good saying about this sort of reductive explanation of other people's ways of thinking: 'For a mistake, that's too big.' Belief in a supernatural world has been too important to too many people for too long to be so easily disposed of. We need a more substantial explanation than has so far been offered.

Here is an illustration suggesting one form such an explanation might take. In the black townships around Johannesburg during the apartheid years there lived tens of thousands of very poor black people who were not allowed to live in, or even close to, the city where they worked. They commuted by train, and it was common for someone to travel back and forth from home for up to two hours each way, each working day. People were not citizens of the city in which they spent much of their time and earned their income, but lived instead in a state of extreme and literal 'alienation'.

Many of these people were members of Zion churches. The church's teaching assured them that although to the carnal eye they might seem to be utterly alienated from the earthly city in which they worked, there was a blessed heavenly city, Zion, of which they could be full citizens, already and all the time, now. By dwelling imaginatively in the heavenly city all day long they could sing and be happy, and could overcome by faith the wretched conditions of their earthly existence. Better still, after death they really would be living in the heavenly city all the time, so that their faith would then be conclusively vindicated.

Since we live in, and have come to take entirely for granted, what are by a very long way the most comfortable, secure and culturally rich circumstances human beings have ever known, it is now very difficult to imagine how hard life used to be for all or very nearly all people. They lived in a state of near-total ignorance and powerlessness. Without knowledge of or control over Nature, people lived under constant and imminent threat from natural disasters, famine, disease, accident and fellow humans. Lives were very short: as late as 1800 the average expectation of life in Britain was around 29 years, in 1900 48 years, in 2000 almost 80 years, and it has recently been reported that if present social conditions and trends can be maintained, then healthy children born today may expect to live around 100 years. *Or more*; and it should be pointed out that over most of the Third World today enough of modern medicine and public health practice has reached people to ensure that their life-expectancy figures are not very far behind the West's. Only in failed states are the life-expectancy statistics as poor today as they were in Britain in 1900.

Until the day before yesterday life for most people was harder than we can now easily imagine. But do not suppose that I am asserting that we should regard religious belief simply as a compensatory fantasy that was necessary in order to make life bearable. No: it was that, but it was also much more than that. Consider the case of cosmology. In the earliest times the world appeared as a theatre in which extremely violent non-rational forces contended ceaselessly with each other. But as religious thought developed, those mythic forces gradually became mythic beings, then powers, and then true *spirits* distinct from, and with knowledge of and power over, the sites with which they were associated. The spirits became gods, and the gods in due course became an organized, sovereign body controlled by an ancient sky-father, who himself then gradually developed towards being the One Nature-transcending God of monotheism, and when full monotheism is reached, all Nature is seen as being subject to a single regime of law. Now, understand that in this whole story we humans were certainly not merely indulging in a compensatory fantasy. No: we were gradually and in theological form developing the all-important idea that there could be, and even that there already was, a unified, law-governed, intelligible and

31

even controllable cosmic order out there; and correspondingly that there could be an autonomous, mobile, self-possessed, rationally unified kind of self that stands back a little from nature, knows all that is happening, and can guide and control events in order to secure the fulfilment of its purposes. If God can be such a self, then perhaps by getting closer to him *we* can get to be like that, too.

In fact we needed to have many, many thousands of years of slow theological development in order to develop all the ideas about the world, unity, order, law, sovereignty, property, knowledge, control, and about a planned course of action to fulfil a purpose; and also the ideas about a moral order, and about degrees of wrongdoing and punishment; and also ideas about being a self that is unified and rational, that knows it is in a world and also is able to stand back a little from the world; a self that has a 'body' in the very broad sense of having a range of ways of expressing itself, influencing events, and securing the fulfilment of its purposes: all this huge range of ideas we first had to develop in religious form before they could be taken over and used by philosophy and then by science. Remember, the earliest humans were desperately weak beings, confronted by overwhelmingly powerful and incomprehensible natural forces. Their technology was minimal: they could nap a flint to make a simple knife, they had harnessed fire and could cook meat, they had perhaps brought home one or two orphaned young animals from the hunt, and had raised and domesticated them. They had some social institutions and skills. But they hardly had any unified, rational, reflective selfhood of their own, and they could not make any progress until they had developed more organized, unified, law-abiding conceptions of the world, society and the self. They were too hard-pressed to be able to do any of these things directly: they had to do them 'heterologously', through religion. It was religious thought that first drafted and then slowly clarified our ideas about the world, about law, about reason, and about active selfhood. Religious ideas such as the idea of God have functioned as regulative ideals for us to aspire after: *we too* could become unified and capable subjects; *we too* could learn how to know the world and reshape our environment to meet our own needs.

And so it happened. Over some thousands of years God created us in his own image, as the idea of God gradually called into being the modern human self.[43] The process is reaching a sort of completion when in the Hebrew Bible we see great heroes of faith such as Abraham and Job beginning to dispute with God, thereby showing that they are becoming a little bit more critical and self-aware than their god is. They are like sparring teenagers who will before long be stronger and smarter than their parents.

Another indication that God's job is done and that he can now afford to hand over everything to humans and fade himself out is given in the teaching of Jesus – and not least in the striking saying: 'And why do you not judge for yourselves what is right?' (Q/Luke 12.57, Kloppenborg[44]). We have now come to the time when we know that ethics is only human. We have eaten the forbidden fruit and have acquired the knowledge of good and evil. We can no longer live under the rule of religious law. We have become wise and self-conscious. We must wear fig leaves and conceal ourselves. From now on we are mortal humans, a little embarrassed, and condemned to history. And God (in Genesis) behaves rather well: he knows this parting must take place, and thoughtfully dresses our first parents in animal skins, which make more effective and functional clothing than those rather silly 'aprons' made of fig leaves.[45]

Have you not previously noticed that the Bible, from its first chapters to its last, is not about how God binds us eternally to himself, but about how God gradually completes his work of bringing *homo sapiens sapiens*, fully modern human beings, into existence so that he can fade himself out? God did make us in his own image in that it was through the slow development of religious thought over a very long period that we were able to forge, *and to build into ourselves*, all our deepest ideas about the world, the self, reason, knowledge, action and ethics. God's sovereignty over Nature was the forerunner of all our ideas about science and technology, God's judgement was the forerunner of all our ideas about critical thinking, and God's lordship over history gave us our first ideas about the possibility of finding a point of view from which modern history could be written. Theological history was the necessary parent of our critical history. So in a certain sense we owe everything to God, and ought to go on believing in God (in a way) long after the death of God. There never actually *was* a god, but that doesn't matter because in these matters that sort of ontological worry is now a waste of time. What does matter is our new postmodern realization that we couldn't have got where we are today *without* God. So we should feel grateful to God, and honour the past to which we owe everything. Indeed, we should love the god who over many millennia fully created us, and himself died in doing so. God died for us; he really did. He deserves commemoration.

7

The Return of God as Self-Decentring Spirit

Twenty-five centuries ago, the first philosophers were people who found the ever-changing and often chaotic flux of our ordinary experience to be intellectually unsatisfying, and considered that the religious myths taught in the temples did little or nothing to clarify matters. They felt that they would be satisfied if they could understand the passing show of things as being grounded in and proceeding from some underlying First Principle or *Arche*.[46] Thus from the first, reflective, intellectual persons tended to equate the making of intellectual progress with a move from surface to depth, from complex to simple, from ever-changing and merely relative appearances to One Thing, absolute, unchanging and self-identical that underlay everything. That One would be the goal of all enquiry, for it would be completely self-explaining and would also be the ultimate explanation of everything else. It would be perfect.

From the first, then, philosophers wanted to move from the Many to the One. They evidently expected to find great intellectual happiness in contemplating the One: it would be ultimately Real, a metaphysical fixture. As that upon which everything rests, it would give the mind rest. But notice that in order to feel completely happy the philosopher needs to feel that he can understand something at least of why and how the One has gone out into, or has brought into being, the Many. If the One is infinite, perfect, self-sufficient and just on its own a supremely satisfying object of attention, why does there have to be anything else at all? At least we can note that if philosophical enquiry is set up along these lines, it is likely to end by disparaging everything other than the One as being 'the world', Vanity Fair, a frivolous distraction. It is also likely to privilege the idea of substance, associating it with unchanging integrity and self-identity. To keep its perfection, the One needs to remain timeless and alone. The empirical world of our everyday experience? – slummy, cluttered and unreal. If the One is the all-inclusive Absolute, then it can surely leave no room for the co-existence, somehow 'alongside' itself, of anything relatively independent of itself. There seems no space for the Many to be anything but a tempting illusion.

An interesting suggestion is sometimes made here. The Absolute is usually thought of as being scarcely more than semi-conscious, lost in a dream of itself. Since it is infinite and simple, it can have no internal structure; there cannot be any distinction within it between the thinker and the thought, the subject and the object of consciousness; and this suggests a reason why the Absolute or Brahman may come to be thought of as needing to go out into plurality. 'The Absolute needs to cast a shadow in order to see its own shape.' The Absolute eternally moves out into plurality in order eternally to recollect itself and return into itself enriched, and more conscious of itself. Hegel's great cosmic myth has something of this form.

Alternatively, suppose that the One be seen as the One God of developed metaphysical monotheism. Here God is Nature-transcending spirit, infinite Mind, highly conscious and spoken of in personal terms. But just because God is spoken of in quasi-personal terms, there is already more than a hint of internal differentiation within God, though whether that differentiation is 'essential' or merely 'economic' is disputed, and the question of why or how God should wish to create anything other than himself remains very awkward. The God of classical metaphysical theism is absolutely perfect, and is 'all-out', being already everything, everywhere, eternally. He is in no respect unfulfilled, and has no needs. Anything God creates must be less than himself, and therefore relatively imperfect; and, what is even worse, God must in some respect limit himself in order to allow anything other than himself some degree of semi-independent reality 'alongside' himself. Creation is therefore a comedown: so why does God create? It appears that *logically* God can have no good reason for creating anything.

The standard reply is that God creates out of pure self-communicating, self-scattering love and generosity. He wants an audience, a theatre for his glory.

To many critics, this suggests that the world is to God pretty much what the Festspielhaus at Bayreuth was to Richard Wagner – a vanity project. God is thirsty for praise, so he creates an audience. To avoid that suggestion, the language needs to be tweaked: it has to be said that God is love, that is, God is pure self-scattering, self-giving generosity. But this line of talk needs to be meant and taken seriously, *really* seriously. In which case the metaphysical theism that pictured God as solitary, self-hugging absolute Being, concerned to defend his own integrity, and distancing himself eternally from everything that is not himself – that kind of theism has been and must be abandoned. To say that *God is love* is in the end to be forced also to admit the converse, that *Love is God*, because in your religious value-scale agapeistic, selfless love is the highest value. We must all of us in the end die for it, and that includes God himself. In and by his act of creation, God commits himself to death. To love is to be vulnerable: if God loves, then God is mortal.

So we arrive at another way in which God returns in postmodernity. In postmodern thought the physical universe no longer has a strong founding Centre that holds it together. Nor does language. Nor does the everyday human life-world. On the contrary, the world and language are everywhere unbounded, proliferating, self-scattering. Everything endlessly pours out and scatters, passing away. Associations and connections ramify endlessly, as in a long-running soap opera. Nothing is a fixture: we are all of us dispensable.

At this point the endless 'dissemination' of modern culture and communications reminds us of some features of traditional theology. At Pentecost, God seems to cease to be infinite substance: he 'pours himself out' like a liquid, 'upon all flesh'. He 'de-centres' himself. At the Last Supper Jesus seems to enact in anticipation the coming fragmentation of his own body and the outpouring of his blood into the little community that he will leave behind him at his death. All of us human persons eventually become scattered into the others whom we leave. In the famous prayer in the *Didache*, the bread is pictured as having been first disseminated as wheat growing on the hillsides, and then as having been gathered to make this loaf. Now it is to be scattered again into the bodies of those present, who look forward to their final gathering into the eschatological Kingdom. Here it seems that a rhythm, a cyclical movement of gathering and scattering, diaspora/dispersal and return, was an important theme in early Christian thought, as it was (and remains) in Jewish thought.

This discussion suggests that there is indeed a strong analogy between the theme of dissemination in postmodern thought, and a similar theme in biblical and early Christian thought. In Christian thought the God of Jesus Christ is, arguably, not an unchanging metaphysical substance, but one who continually decentres and scatters himself, giving himself away, dying into us. The principal Christian rite, the Eucharist, is a repeated enactment of exactly this theme: the Sacred becomes human among us, and passes out into us, just as we too have to tread the same path. I am somewhat more than middle-aged at the time of writing, and am rapidly passing away into the kinsfolk, the friends and the written words that I will soon be leaving behind eternally. I must remain solar as I go the way of all flesh; for God has become man, not in order to ensure that we will live for ever, but in order to show us how to live a dying life. In the postmodern rewriting of Christianity there is no longer any eternal Being out there, and there is no postmodern Volume Two of our lives: instead, the Death of God shows us how to die, how to 'make the sacrifice complete'.[47] On this account, God is not an

38

infinite substance, but simply self-outpouring process, like the Cosmos, and like solar living.

If so, why did early Christianity reinstate metaphysics and religious law, and develop into a religion of eternal salvation in the heavenly world after death? Because it was born into a very precarious and extremely violent world in which it appeared that absolute monarchy was the normal and necessary form of government. World-view, morality, law and social control had to be very strongly *centred*. Or so it appeared, and the counter-movement of decentring or anarchism has resurfaced only in modern times, with the transition from monarchy to democracy, and the struggles for all-round human emancipation from life under authority.

This suggests that if the current political situation had been different, Christianity might from the beginning have taken a very different form. In the religion as we know it, the two chief metaphysical convictions on which all else rests are the traditional strongly 'centred' or 'realistic' beliefs, in God and in God's finite counterpart, the immortal rational soul in man. The whole faith is understood as quest for eternal security, and the 'hypostatic union' of the two natures, divine and human, in Christianity is the basis on which people believe (or used to believe) that they could be, and already were, joined eternally to God in Christ without confusion. The infinite difference between the divine and the human remains eternally, but Christ bridges the chasm for everyone.

Now, however, we see the possibility of an entirely different Christian religion. There is no metaphysic of substantial, independent being. Instead, religion celebrates transience, scattering, and passing away, as universal cosmic process and, *moralized*, as self-decentring and ecstatic love. At the cosmic level, the symbol for this is God; and at the human level, Christ. Christ is not a metaphysical being, but a process of self-giving; for in Christianity the Sacred has migrated above all into the field of human personal relationships, *philadelphia*. So again, the Eucharist enacts the affirmations of transience and of self-giving which in the Christian view are the basis of the good society.[48]

So we simply do without the traditional concern for metaphysical realism, for personal security, for authority and for absolutes, for 'orthodoxy', and for spiritual power. We keep *only* endless scattering, dissemination, and pure agapeistic love of life and of the neighbour. We repeatedly celebrate only that: it is all we need. And, of course, it is all there is.

8

The Return of God as Judge in Critical Thinking

At some time in the late 1970s I was reading and puzzling over the philosophy of religion then being put forward by Dewi Z. Phillips, of Swansea and then later of Claremont, California. Phillips sometimes appealed to Kierkegaard as a previous holder of his own non-realist view of God, so I thought of trying an experiment. I read Kierkegaard's famously stringent and relentless essay in self-examination, *Purity of Heart is to Will One Thing* (1846) slowly and carefully from the non-realist point of view. That is, I imagined that for Kierkegaard God was perhaps not a real being, a Heavenly Father who was looking critically into his heart, but rather was simply 'the standpoint of Eternity', an ideal point of view from which I might feel myself to be judged absolutely. Could *Purity of Heart* be read from this angle, seeing God as an ideal standard for self-assessment rather than as a being?

It could, and my little experiment converted me to the non-realist point of view.[49] The ideas involved here are not difficult. In Greek, *krinō*, I judge, and *krisis*, judgement, imply sifting, discerning, and carrying out a thorough and systematic enquiry or trial, and there is obviously not all that wide a gap between being examined by God, and examining one's own conscience *as if* before God. The Scottish poet Robert Burns links the two in the oft-quoted lines:

O wad some Power the giftie gie us
To see oursels as ithers see us![50]

In the biblical tradition people were conscious of God as a judge who searched human hearts, and before whom they would have to appear at the Last Day. Others in the Greek tradition quoted the maxim 'Know thyself!', and practised self-examination in the hope of achieving a calmer and more unified selfhood. People who lack self-knowledge often do not realize how comical they may appear in the eyes of others – as, for example, Jesus points out when mocking the Pharisees' self-righteousness, and their love of fine clothes and the best seats in the synagogues.[51] Such people really need more self-awareness.

So in the Western tradition critical thinking was at first chiefly a moral discipline. One pursued self-knowledge by self-criticism, or by examining one's conscience before God the Judge. The idea was that by thorough self-questioning one could bring to light one's own groundless assumptions, gaps in self-awareness, and self-deceptions.[52] By this method one could hope to make steady progress in building or in becoming a better and more clear-sighted self. Thus critical thinking was from the first not just a one-off test procedure. It involved a way of life from which one never retired: one was supposed to strive continually for betterment throughout one's life. The self is a slippery customer, and the work of purifying it takes a very long time.

How far self-examination and a strict penitential discipline really does and can succeed in making one a better *person* may be disputed. But what is beyond doubt is that the programme of a rigorous and systematic examination in order to search out and expunge errors, mistaken assumptions and self-deceptions, all in pursuit of greater integrity, consistency, clarity and perhaps efficiency in the way one does things, and linked with a determination to continue indefinitely in actually seeking to reform and to progress – this programme has potentially explosive effects if it is applied on a large scale to our knowledge, our institutions and our practices. It is sure in the end to break out of the old tradition-directed kind of society in which everyone instinctively defends received knowledge and ways of doing things, and to create instead a new kind of society committed to endless progressive growth and improvement.[53]

In Western Europe at the Reformation the criticism of tradition and of its chief guardian, the Bishop of Rome, did begin, and with a bang. The work of Erasmus, Luther, Copernicus and many others triggered a huge explosion of cultural change and of new critically tested knowledge, at first mainly in history and then in the natural sciences. The extraordinarily rapid growth of new knowledge, new technologies and new wealth still continues and has now swept across the entire planet.

There are reservations, however. As we remarked, the self is a slippery customer, and it is not at all clear how we can be sure of success in the pursuit of a moral discipline of progressive self-examination, reform and improvement. Where do we get the criteria from, and how do we measure success in fulfilling them? And in the case of *social* progress there are similar problems, for we may not find it easy to establish agreed rational criteria for a good society. New technologies – for example, in medicine – that at first seemed obviously beneficial may eventually lead to an unsustainable population surge and a very painful crash. One person's progress may be another's decline; and if on philosophical grounds we have been led to a radical-humanist and *historicist* vision of the world, then we may suddenly recognize that we do not have and never will have moral and political standards that are fully independent of history and of our own criticism. In which case, the whole idea of progress breaks down – as happened in the philosophy of Nietzsche.

Today, we are still living in the Nietzschean epoch. We do not have, and we clearly understand why we cannot have, any guiding vision or moral or intellectual standards that are permanently authoritative and quite independent of ourselves and our history. We seem to be sunk in relativism or, as others call it, 'nihilism'. The same critical spirit that has brought us to this position is also quite unpersuaded by the various forms of authoritarian politics and fundamentalist religion that have been touted and that briefly flourished during the twentieth century.

Nothing is left to us but the critical spirit itself. Currently it goes under various names in the various fields in which it operates: journalistic freedom, the independence of the judiciary, academic freedom, 'good science' and 'peer review' – in the broad sense of being guided by the conversational consensus among recognizably qualified people in the same subject area. The chief guardians of the critical spirit are the great learned societies such as the Royal Society, and the principal professional bodies. Those lay persons who are nowadays called 'whistle-blowers' also deserve a mention here.

Most rigorous of all are the 'thirty-six hidden saints' of critical thinking who are to be found among the strictest critical scholars, philosophers and scientists. In Jewish legend, with an allusion to Genesis 18.22–23, it was said that at any one time there are thirty-six hidden saints for whose sake God permits the world to continue in existence; and I am suggesting that today everything depends upon the very small number of people who really are completely dedicated to the critical spirit. It is like an immanent god dwelling within them, and today it is all we human beings have left to us.

Someone who lives by and for the true critical spirit is someone who is dedicated to the very highest intellectual standards and who then goes even higher, because he constantly questions, criticizes and revises those standards themselves. He, or she, is ultra-scrupulous: 'his own severest critic' or 'hardest taskmaster', as people say. The person whom he finds it hardest of all to satisfy is himself.

Such people are very rare indeed, and their religion is a very demanding one. But they do exist: many but not all of them are philosophers, and some are scientists or lawyers. They are saints of a kind, and the critical spirit in them is a return of God as Judge.

9

The Return of Divine Grace in Universal Contingency

In the brightness of the world of our visual experience we may see a return of the divine glory, and in much the same way we may experience the sheer contingency of everything as divine grace. In the former case, the glory is a kind of charisma, glow, or radiance spread across the visual field, but it is free-floating: it is not anybody's glory, and appears rather to be an effect of language. Similarly, in the latter case we may experience our own life's sheer contingency, or perhaps its renewal after a bad period, as grace, a pure gift or bonus that is all the more wonderfully gracious or gratuitous for having no giver.

The sense that our life is a gift is particularly strong when we have a narrow escape from death by accident, disaster or severe illness, or when we find ourselves passing the age of 70 and still in tolerably good health and spirits. 'I'm grateful to life,' we may say, resolving henceforth to be carefree. The extra lease of life is pure bonus, extra time, something just thrown in. We should make the most of it, by living generously.

It is a curious fact that although the typically postmodern world-view is so very firmly post-metaphysical, post-theistic, and even nihilistic, a great deal of religion that used to be strictly supernatural somehow returns into it – albeit in a new guise. There is an example of this in the most important lineage of British artists to emerge in the last half-century. Francis Bacon, Gilbert and George, and Damien Hirst are all very 'black': they come from the tradition of Beckett,

Sartre and atheistic existentialism. But there remains a good deal of preoccupation with traditional religious subjects and religious language in their work: most notably, crucifixes, death and transience. They are almost late-Baroque Catholics, like Warhol. And something very similar may be said about the work in the USA of the painters Barnett Newman, Mark Rothko and Ad Reinhardt. Even in Reinhardt's plain black squares, a ghostly cross-shape still hovers dimly. Religious ideas and symbols are most evidently tenacious and powerful when they return so conspicuously in contexts from which they should have been finally eliminated. Newman called a very austere series of black-and-white abstracts *Stations of the Cross*, and Hirst has at least one crucified skeleton.

How does pure 'meaningless' contingency (or befalling, or accident) suddenly turn into pure grace, in the sense of a favour, an unmerited blessing? From the Latin *gratus*, 'pleasing', 'thankful', and *gratia*, 'grace', 'kindness' we get in English a large number of cognate terms, but a simple way of bringing out the main contrast is by comparing 'gratuitous' with 'gratuity'. In contemporary English, what is gratuitous is something that is contingent, in the sense of being not just unexpected, but uncalled-for, even unwelcome, and sometimes 'free of charge'. But a gratuity carries a much stronger positive meaning: it is a tip, a favour, something superadded, and it is to be accepted as a pleasant surprise.

The same sort of range of meanings is found among the cognates of hap, luck and *fors*/fortune.[54] 'Hap' is archaic now: it means fate, or fortune, or it may be any chance event, considered as a happening, as happenstance, or as a mishap. But if the contingencies of life 'happen' to turn out well for us, then we may be made happy. Hap has turned out very happily, like a fortunate coincidence.

Luck and *fors*, or fortune, behave similarly. What's a matter of luck is sheerly contingent, and we have no way of ensuring in advance that we will have good luck, or be 'lucky', rather than have bad luck. As for *fors*, fortune, it gives us the word 'fortuitous', which is very similar to 'gratuitous': it means unplanned, happening by chance and not by design. But in recently popular spoken usage 'fortuitous' has come to be used in the same sense as fortunate – and so, like 'fortunate' itself, has come to suggest only a *happy* chance, as distinct from a misfortune. It seems that we now actually like living in a contingent world, and are inclined to take a hopeful view of what it may bring.

Finally, we may briefly recall words that compare eventuality or occurrence with the falling of a die, or with the chance 'coming' of something. They include befall, accident and incident (from *cadere*, to fall), and such beautiful idioms as 'it came to pass' and 'it came about that'.

There is a remarkable range of idioms which shows how ordinary language now regards the going-on of things in the world of experience as being purely contingent and unforeseeable. It also shows how closely we all examine what is happening to us in the hope, perhaps, of finding that we are 'having a run of good luck' and 'fortune is smiling on us'. If indeed it is 'your lucky day', then perhaps you will be able to 'ride your luck', making the most of it while it lasts.

All this may suggest that among ordinary people a pagan belief in a capricious goddess of fortune still survives, but others protest in an almost Kantian vein that those who are diligent, skilled and persistent 'make their own luck'. They have earned their luck.

We have found a strangely large collection of idioms about the contingency of life. They are so numerous that it would seem that we have now completely lost the old predestinarian belief, firmly rooted in biblical thought, that there is no such thing as chance or luck. In those days, all events were seen as predestined by God and as taking place in fulfilment of his great moral purpose, the Plan of Salvation. Even at times when we cannot immediately make sense of it all we should still soldier on, in the faith that in retrospect things presently dark will be made to look brighter. 'God is his own interpreter, and he will make it plain'.

All that, we seem to have lost. Instead, the way things have gone for us, the lives we have lived and the things we have done – all that seems to be purely contingent, and things might have 'turned out' very differently for us. I am not, it seems, solely responsible for what I am. Some of what I am I have brought upon myself, but the rest has just happened to me.

Because of this change, the problem of evil – 'Why did God let it happen?', and 'Why *me*?' – bulks much less large in people's thinking than it used to. Some people are lucky, and some people are unlucky, and that is all there is to say. Nobody has got it in for me, and I don't have to worry about divine wrath. It is many, many years since I last heard somebody express the fear that she or he had committed the unforgivable sin and was doomed. I am now at an age when my friends are beginning one by one to succumb, each to their own last illness. A few of them still feel emotionally the old rage: 'Why *me*?' But they all know that this is not *a question* that they can expect to be answered, but an emotional reaction that they've got to work through. And many now realize that it is a blessing no longer to have to believe that one's illness is 'a divine visitation'. It is a blessing to be free now from the old terrible fear that one is a damned soul, heading for hell. I'm happy to think that almost nobody now even remembers what a dreadful fear the fear of damnation once was. It is a comfort to think that although we have indeed lost many of the consolations of religion, we have also lost its former terrors.

In this new context, just life itself seems to be a great blessing while we have it. Just to welcome each morning, just to see once more the annual cycle of plant and animal life, and just to feel the sun and to know that one is still able to enjoy life – all this remains a blessing, an unlooked-for gift, a happy happening. Just life itself makes *me* feel as happy as his personal Assurance of Salvation used to make the old Calvinist feel.

Strange: ordinary people now feel, and I feel, that the sheer gratuitousness or contingency of everything is – for most of the time – more gracious than the old Moral Providence ever was. It's wrong to call contingency 'meaningless': we like it.

10

The Return of the Cosmic Christ in Radical Humanism

Around 50,000 years ago humans became anatomically capable of speech, but some think that it was not until about 20,000 years ago that we were psychologically ready for speech. We are not yet sure of the dates, but when human beings first acquired language and a moderately unified kind of consciousness and looked about them, what could they see and how might they understand the human situation?[55]

Remember that neither they nor we have any reason a priori to expect to find *either* an objective, ready-made, extra-human real world, *or* an only-human world constructed by human language as it battles to impose order upon the chaos of experience. To put it briefly, we don't know in advance whether we have only *our own* human life-world, or whether we have *the* world, an independently real cosmos all laid on for us.

So how did the human situation look to the first humans? It seemed to them that they were very weak. They had no theory, and their vocabulary was too poor for them to have any hope of being able to *master* the world by describing it thoroughly. Instead it seemed to them that they were like ants caught up in a rugby scrum. They were surrounded by mysterious and overwhelming powers and forces that seemed to care little about human beings. Sometimes it was as if the Powers were kind to humans, and sometimes they casually destroyed us.

How were these early humans to make any progress? They did have sight of some regularities: the daily cycle of the sun, the monthly cycles of the moon and of women, the annual cycles of the seasons and of plant and animal life. At least some regulation of human life by customary law began early. So, in order to develop a better cosmology, humans needed first to do theology and then to bring human life under the control of a system of religious law. Doing theology involved gradually learning to think of the Powers as invisible quasi-personal beings, distinct from the various cosmic regions that they controlled. The Powers became organized into a society with a definite power-structure. An ancient sky-father unified the whole pantheon and was the source of natural law. Gradually religion evolved towards ethical monotheism, as the notion of a law-governed and generally friendly world of Nature developed. And in the whole of this long history human beings were gradually opening up the same possibilities *for themselves*. First they imagined the gods doing something and then they began to learn how to do it themselves. We too could learn gradually to order and control the world. The gods blazed a trail, and then humans could follow them along it. Remember Hegel's famous chapter on the Master–Servant relationship: watching the Master closely and doing his will diligently, the Servant eventually becomes fully the equal of the Master, and is ready to take over.

There are many indications that it has been through the history of religions that human beings have gradually developed and unified themselves and their world. In the first place, the gods themselves gradually become a kind of upper class of 'lords', with close analogies between different kinds of 'service' – domestic, royal and divine. Note that humanism is reached when these early kinds of service give way to *public* service. Second, the gods gradually cease to appear on earth in person, instead handing over to the human voice and to writing – that is, to prophets and to scriptural writers and interpreters. Third, colossal human figures crop up in many of the world's principal religions, perhaps as symbols of a possible future human greatness.[56] In some Indian traditions – Hindu and Jain – the cosmos itself is seen in human form.

Even in sixteenth-century Europe there are still detailed astrological and other correspondences between the cosmos and the human body, indicating that the world is man's and for man. Fourth, in the Hebrew Bible and elsewhere there seems to be a progressive handover by God of his powers to human beings. God recognizes from the beginning that we will eventually be taking over from him. In the New Testament Jesus of Nazareth seems to be telling humans that it is now time for them to become fully autonomous in ethics, and to break free from the old government of life by revealed divine law.[57] This process reaches a certain culmination when Jesus actually becomes Christos Pantocrator in early Christian art. An historical man is seated on the throne of the universe. He signifies the complete appropriation and familiarization of the world by humans, first achieved in and by him. He has actually overcome the old Powers.

Although modern radical humanism was from the first implicit in Christianity (and also perhaps in some other traditions too) it comes out into the open and becomes fully conscious of itself only in the nineteenth century in Comte, in Ludwig Feuerbach and the young Karl Marx, in Nietzsche and, in its American form, in William James and F. C. S. Schiller. The crucial philosophical arguments stem from Kant, whose 'Copernican Revolution' marks the changeover from heterologous to autologous thinking. After Kant there are always going to be people who recognize that the only world there is for us is *our* world, a world shaped by our interests, our ways of thinking, our theories and our point of view – in short, by our *language*. We give the orders: we wrote the physics textbooks, and we did not discover, but in every case we *invented*, the laws of nature and made them work. So the world is ours, really ours, and there is no longer any non-human being, visible or invisible, who has the power to threaten either our way of building our world or our values. Which is something to be really happy, *eternally* happy, about.

That's radical humanism, and I am suggesting that in it we can recognize a return of a religious image not much invoked nowadays, namely the image of the regnant Christ seated on the firmament or on a rainbow with a gold nimbus or halo behind his head. It is necessary here to remember that the major monotheistic faiths were *all* of them very wary of images of God. During the first millennium of Christianity God the Father was never portrayed in Michelangelo's way, as something like an old man. On the contrary, the Church stuck strictly to the maxim that so far at least as this world is concerned the only human form under which God appears and is knowable is the form of the man Jesus Christ. And when we fully understand this last point we begin to see that as belief in the real existence of a higher invisible world beyond this world begins to fade, Christianity must evolve into radical religious humanism. As it has done.

Interestingly, the devil began to be portrayed not as a grotesque but as a beautiful human during the fifteenth century. The crucial work is a portrayal of the expulsion of Lucifer from heaven in the *Tres Riches Heures* of the *Duc de Berry*.[58] Lucifer is tall, crowned, handsome, golden-haired and dressed in a long blue robe. He's human, and from now on he remains human. God the Father first began to be portrayed in human form at about the same time, no doubt because Byzantium had fallen and, with the rediscovery of a good deal of pagan classical literature, the Renaissance version of humanism had become established. People were ceasing to believe in a non-human supernatural world-above and were turning to an anthropocentric world-view that contrasted Man the microcosm or little world with Nature the macrocosm or great world, and then explored astrological connections between the two. All of which is hokum: but it shows how the old supernaturalism, as it died, was giving birth to humanism.

11

The Return of the Sacred

In Nikolaus Pevsner's celebrated series of architectural guides to the buildings, first of England and then of the entire British Isles, a standard format was established from the outset and is still maintained. *The sacred comes first*: in every human settlement Pevsner treats first, religious buildings, second, other public architecture, and then all other architecture, commercial, recreational and domestic.

In this, Pevsner follows a very ancient tradition which maintains that every important human settlement has been built around a spot where people have had dealings with the Sacred. In the most important cases of all, this central place is believed to be the site where the god established his Presence and his habitation in the earliest times. Perhaps he actually ordered creation from this site, which first appeared as a small mound or hillock when the Primal Flood receded.

At any rate Pevsner, although personally secular, regarded the church as being still the premier building in every settlement, despite the long, slow process of secularization that has been going on in Europe since the late Middle Ages. Once, almost every learned person was a *clericus*, clerk or member of the clergy, the *clerici*, and the Church controlled most of the culture. But gradually one institution after another was secularized, or removed from church control. Rates of religious observance fell, and the Church's former power and wealth declined. And this long-drawn-out process of secularization appears to have accelerated since the 1960s. The increasing disuse and the vandalization of church buildings (and the felt need, therefore, to keep them locked) is one sign of it.

Another is the secularization of Sunday, now at last becoming complete after a hard-fought rearguard action.

As a result of this whole process, there seems now to be a very large number of people who have entirely *forgotten* the Sacred. It no longer exists for them at all. Not even death reminds them of it: funeral and memorial services have become surprisingly secular, and 'woodland burials' are for many replacing the old interment in consecrated ground. Instead of praying, we now utter such formulae as: 'Our thoughts are with you at this difficult time.' Even life after death is, it seems, being forgotten. It is mentioned only to children.

Yet, paradoxically, the postmodern culture that has accelerated the decline of the Sacred has also seen its return in a whole series of new forms. They seem to include at least the following four: art (especially music), the sublime in landscape, personal *charisma*, and 'icons'.

The Sacred has 'migrated', to use the standard metaphor. There was an amusing example of this in mid-eighteenth-century Germany, when the last architectural style of the old 'great' religious tradition, namely late-Baroque with rich Rococo decoration, suddenly came to an end. Rococo illusionism seemed too frivolous, and clients were demanding serious neo-Classicism instead. But somehow an after-echo of the Rococo style survived in the architecture of entertainment, and opera houses, music halls and cinemas remained visibly post-Rococo until as late as the 1930s. Furthermore, picture frames, ornate and gilded, remain similarly post-Rococo to this day in art galleries around the world, and perhaps appropriately, because a visit to an art gallery has for so many people become a solemn occasion, a little like 'going to church', an occasion where artists do what priests used to do, namely re-*mind* us of, and help us to engage with, the depths of life, its boundaries, its fundamental conditions and its extremes.

As for music, is it not the case that we who are not musically gifted envy those who are, because they have much easier and more frequent access than we do to the wellsprings of religious feeling? As the culture has become more secular it has become steadily more difficult to 'do religion' convincingly in architecture, or in cinema, or indeed in most of the arts; but music has been able to remain religious. In the older generation at least, a large number of composers are still clearly religious in style and temperament. Of which other art can that be said? Perhaps the reason for this is that music is more directly and clearly emotivist and 'non-cognitive' than other arts, and therefore can continue to be unabashedly religious in an age when most people are aware that no religious doctrine is (in the old strong sense) actually True. In this climate, where we have little or no intellectual access to religion, music is the best and most innocent doorway to religious feeling that we have. We don't have to commit our heads to it: only our hearts.

Music has been closely associated with religion from the very earliest times, especially because of its power literally to *entrance* – that is, to throw people into an altered state of consciousness.[60] The case of landscape is very different, because it has seen so sharp a reversal of valuations. Despite harbouring so much human poverty, crime and disease, the city was always in the past the place with God's house at its centre, a place of pilgrimage to which one went 'seeking the face of God'. The wilderness was the home of demons, and holy men went out there 'to be tempted by the devil'. Then, as everyone knows, there was a remarkable reversal of values in the late eighteenth century. The wildest landscapes, especially in mountainous regions, became 'pure', 'virgin' and 'unsullied'. As after Kant the old Transcendent faded away, the sublime in landscape stepped forward to replace it.

There was a genuinely close analogy here. In both cases, whether we are contemplating a vast landscape from a mountain peak, or whether in prayer we are unthinking all the images as we try to approach the thought of God, there is a very similar feeling of dizziness, disorientation and spiritual exaltation: so that to this day mountaineering writers use a secularized religious vocabulary to convey their experiences. They speak, for example, of 'touching the Void'. Neo-orthodox theologians have often protested that the sublime in land-scape is 'merely natural' and is not to be confused with the metaphysical transcendence of God, but the mountaineering writers go on writing, and the public go on reading them.

In England, as in many other European countries, there has been a long tradition of seeking reminders of a lost Eden in what we call 'the countryside', and of trying to recreate Eden, both in the gardens around our houses and also in large botanical gardens. But in this case we have always been aware that the carefully built and maintained paradise-garden is pre-cisely *not* wild. All along it has been consciously a human cul-tural artefact, and therefore is quite different from the Sacred that is sought in mountain regions, or in the loneliness of a long sea voyage by single-handed sailors in yachts.

The relocation of the Sacred in art – especially music – and in landscape is by now very well established. Much more recent is the popular adulation of 'charismatic' celebrities or 'stars', which resembles the cult of saints and has become highly developed especially in the advanced countries, and especially in connection with the cinema. There were a few nineteenth-century international stars – Byron, Dickens, Tolstoy – but twentieth-century stardom depended upon very active com-mercial promotion of the star's image, which could now easily be disseminated on a global scale. The early names best remembered are perhaps those of Chaplin, Valentino, Douglas Fairbanks and Mary Pickford, and Garbo. So great was their impact that similar techniques of promotion were used to sustain a generation of political dictators: but the Great Dictators are now (almost all of them) dead, while the star system continues to be as popular as ever. In India, the travel-ling painter-signwriters who used to paint images of the gods on great public billboards changed over easily to producing posters for Bollywood cinema in the same style – exactly the same transition as the one made at the end of the Rococo style, and clear evidence that the world of popular stars is today's recycling *within a radical-humanist culture* of the old supernatural world of religion. The stars are our ideals, the people we wish we could be, and we hope, by cult-ivating them and by mimicking them, gradually to become more like them. As for the word *charisma*, it was popularized in the early twentieth century by Max Weber, who contrasted the institutionally validated kind of leadership that is given to all priests with the charismatic kind of leadership that individual figures such as prophets achieve because of their exceptional personal qualities. But of course the word *charisma* is Greek, and in particular it comes from the New Testament, a *charisma* being a special grace freely bestowed by God. Again, what today is called 'star-quality' or 'star-power' is a return within a secular-humanist culture of the old religious notion of a special glow or aura or nimbus that shines from those who are regarded as being specially blessed.

It is against this background that we should understand the sudden vogue – since about 1995, perhaps? – for the Greek word 'icon', used in a new, extended sense.

Historically, an icon was a symbol or image. Christ in the New Testament is spoken of as the visible icon of the invisible God.[61] This was originally shocking, given that the Jews object just as much as Muslims do to any representation of God in human form. But an icon was, or gradually became because of Christ, rather more than a typical specimen or a representative symbol. It seizes and holds your attention, it sticks in the memory, and it is standard-setting or exemplary. Indeed its charismatic power is so great that it overflows onto all other things in its neighbourhood, so much so that a single structure can nowadays instantly bring a whole city to mind. Utzon's great sails say Sydney Opera House, Foster's cigar-shaped tower (the Swiss Re building at 30 St Mary Axe, 'the Gherkin') instantly says London, Gustav Eiffel's Tour says Paris: and film makers use such buildings regularly in 'establishing shots' that tell us immediately where the following action is located.

Historically, an icon was a painted wooden panel, bearing an image of a sacred person or scene. Despite one great and fierce controversy, icons became important devotional objects in Eastern Orthodox Christianity. The most famous modern illustration of their power is the piece of film showing Russian Orthodox priests, at the command of Joseph Stalin, parading icons before lines of troops in order to raise national morale at a desperate time in the Great Patriotic War of the early 1940s.

Perhaps like Stalin, we have suddenly felt an urgent need to bring icons back in recent years, and perhaps especially in the urban world of fashion, design, communications, the media and advertising. Living amidst an overwhelming flood of endlessly multiplied text, imagery and consumer 'products', we seem to be harking back to the pre-industrial age when a single religious image could radiate 'quality' and sacred power. In the modern desert of mediocrity, we would like to be able to identify some such objects – or at least, their modern counterparts: things that radiate sharply individual and standard-setting, enduring, authority and power.

In the East, here and there, I have seen peasant life in which people still have some contact with religious objects of genuine quality. In Western suburbia everything around you in the built environment, and in the contents of the houses, looks as if it was acquired in a garden centre. You can go from house to house all day without seeing anything really good, and indeed without meeting anyone aware of what is missing. Our tendency in recent years to bring back the ancient lost vocabulary of religion surely expresses a wish that we could recreate or rediscover top quality within the flat, democratized, radical-humanist mass culture to which we are now irreversibly committed.

12

The Return of Beatitude
into this Life

It must be confessed that belief in life after death has rarely, if ever, been strong and convincingly spelt out in Western Christianity. No Western philosopher, not even Plato, has ever produced a persuasive argument for it. It is true that there was some discussion of the Beatific Vision in the later Middle Ages, but no very clear popular answer was ever given to such simple questions as: *What exactly is there to see? How is it seen?* and *How can seeing it make us completely happy forever?* Even less of an answer can be given to a slightly more advanced question such as: *If after death we are still ourselves, and still finite, will not God transcend our thought just as much then as he does now?*

The pure Vision of God has never been explained clearly, and perhaps has never been a very popular idea. In medieval art there are the familiar images of people in long gowns walking about a well-kept garden, of a brilliant central Light or an enthronement, of an orchestra and choir, and of a great crowd. In medieval art the crowd is often carefully paraded in distinct classes of people, perhaps in great circles rising in tiers around the central focus; whereas the huge jostling crowd in Tintoretto's *Paradise* is already more levelled and democratic-looking. But none of these images has been considered informative by ordinary people in recent centuries, and by the end of the eighteenth century there is little doubt that if people look to life after death at all, it is in the hope of being reunited with friends and loved ones. The witness of poetry seems to be that that hope died soon after Tennyson's time, and in any case it should be obvious that Scripture and the mainline religious tradition do not in any way encourage the naively eudemonistic idea that the main purpose of life after death is to give us hope that we shall see our loved ones again.

The older and grander idea of the Vision of God lingers in seventeenth-century poetry, and Wordsworth draws upon it in a very fine sonnet of August 1802. He is walking at sundown along the seashore near Calais, accompanied by his daughter Caroline, the child of Annette Vallon:

> It is a beauteous Evening, calm and free;
> The holy time is quiet as a Nun
> Breathless with adoration; the broad sun
> Is sinking down in its tranquillity;
> The gentleness of heaven is on the Sea:
> Listen! The mighty Being is awake
> And doth with his eternal motion make
> A sound like thunder – everlastingly.[62]

In the first section of the poem Wordsworth uses the image of the nun in contemplative prayer to leave us in no doubt that he regards the scene and the mood it brings about in him as religious. But he is always aware of the observer's contribution to what he sees, and he goes on at once to describe the unconscious religiousness of another observer, the eight-year-old who walks beside him:

> Dear Child! dear Girl! that walkest with me here,
> If thou appear'st untouched by solemn thought,
> Thy nature is not therefore less divine:
> Thou liest in Abraham's bosom all the year,
> And worshipp'st at the Temple's inner shrine,
> God being with thee when we know it not.

Now we see that Wordsworth is doing something remarkable in this sonnet: *he is bringing the heavenly world down into*

this world twice over, and from 'opposite directions'. The
adult sees in a slow, calm and magnificent sunset an image of
beatitude, of final happiness and religious fulfilment. Nature
at its grandest heals and almost divinizes the mind that con-
templates it. In the case of the child, Wordsworth harks back
to the traditional Platonic belief in the pre-existence of the
soul in the heavenly world – a belief that he himself knows
to be mythical, but of which he freely makes poetic use anyway[63] in order to say that the eight-year-old's innocent freshness is itself also 'divine'. Thus both the soul's post-life vision
of God and its pre-life in heaven are demythologized in their
different ways and from opposite directions into this moment
now, this evening, as father and daughter walk together by
the sea.

Now, and subtler: in both cases the divinization is brought
about in the mind of the poet himself as he, the observer,
interprets what he sees; and Wordsworth knows this. That is
why in many places he attributes such extraordinary powers
and cosmic significance to the human mind:

> the mind of man . . .
> A thousand times more beautiful than the earth
> On which he dwells, above this Frame of things . . .
> In beauty exalted, as it is itself
> Of substance and of fabric more divine.[64]

Here, though, Wordsworth goes over the top. The beauty, the
divine transformative power, belongs not to his own mind
but to language, which is a common, public creation. It is important to make this last admission, because it 'decentres' the
postmodern self and saves us from the Romantic poet's sin of
personal vanity. Like Milton, Wordsworth was tempted to
regard himself as a superior being.

Now a further, and controversial, line of argument, un-
known I think to Wordsworth himself: because any talk about
the heavenly world must perforce be couched entirely in metaphors drawn from this present world, when we demythologize

such talk and bring it back down into this world, we *cannot* be losing anything – can we?

Let us now reverse the same argument. Nobody has yet produced a satisfactory 'doctrine of analogy'. That is, there is no good theory that explains how, by jiggling words whose ordinary use is purely this-worldly, we can generate real and useful information about how things are in a quite-different supposed heavenly World-Above. How can we possibly be warranted in claiming such a thing, in view of the fact that nobody can go and test the claim and then come back and tell us whether it was indeed warranted?

I conclude that in principle there can be no objection to the modern habit of returning virtually *all* talk of heaven and hell into this life, and using such talk to characterize everyday situations and states of affairs. After all, this life is outsideless and there is no other, and that's where all such talk originally came from. We are not losing anything, because the language was never able anyway genuinely to reach beyond itself, and could never be shown to have succeeded in doing so. The limits of our world and of our language coincide perfectly.

In view of these arguments, then, we return to the original example. The sun is setting in the West on a wonderful summer's evening. Life affords us no grander image of its own end and fulfilment, and talk of 'life after death' cannot possibly give us anything more than that.

Now if we go back to the perennial question about our own cultural epoch, we can ask ourselves this question: 'In post-modernity, nothing remains to us but the human life world, which is and exactly coincides with the world of language. Is postmodernity then unendurably shallow, nihilistic and trivial? Have we lost something which the "great" period of religion knew, and which we might be able to recover?' Or, alternatively, we may reply: 'No, we have not lost anything, for if language really *is* outsideless and we still have language, then everything we ever had must still be available to us within our language.' In which case the essence of religion must still be recoverable within a radical humanist world-view.

And that is precisely what, in these dozen short chapters, we have been trying to show. A surprisingly large amount of traditional religious belief has in fact been quietly returning into our new and purportedly quite secular postmodern culture. It has often returned in strange guise, but religious ideas are notoriously both very tenacious and very flexible. It is therefore surely worth asking how much of traditional religion really *does* come through to us, under postmodern cultural conditions.

13

The Self-Decentring of God

The most important thinker of the 'postmodern' period so far has probably been Jacques Derrida. His philosophy has sometimes been described as 'the Death of God put in writing'. The simplest way to explain this is to say that, following in the footsteps of the psychoanalyst Jacques Lacan, Derrida applied approximately Freudian ways of thinking in a very thoroughgoing manner to literary texts. The resulting highly original philosophy of writing seems to rule out any idea that the everywhere-shifting, ambivalent world of our language needs, or can have, a great master-word, a Founding Centre that anchors and controls everything else. In effect, the Death of God is now seen as following directly from the very nature of language. Language is and has to be fluid, ambivalent, relativistic and unanchored. It pours out, and it passes away. As it passes, it briefly does its job. We say one thing by leaving another thing unsaid: we foreground this, and relegate that to the background. But don't try to pin language down! There cannot be the sort of fixed, original 'real meanings' and foundational truths that many people believe in. It just doesn't work like that.

Derrida's ideas first emerged and gradually became current during the 1960s. Then during the 1970s and 80s his influence became worldwide. During the same years people came generally to recognize that the agenda-setting modern thinker whose influence pervades late Western culture is now no longer Karl Marx, but Friedrich Nietzsche.

The prominence of Nietzsche's name and a flood of new studies of his writings have prompted people to ask just how far back his apparently shocking idea of 'the Death of God' can be traced. Martin Heidegger suggested that Western thought had already left metaphysics behind, and therefore also the classical doctrine of God, in the thought of Karl Marx in the 1840s. Nietzsche himself seems to have associated the Death of God with the period of the French Revolution and the philosophies of Kant and Schopenhauer. Certainly the mainstream of Western culture became post-theistic at that time. While Kant was publishing, the Theology Faculty was still the most powerful faculty in a major German university, but as Schopenhauer grew older that ceased to be true. Heinrich Heine published a famous and much-quoted essay about God's deathbed.[65]

There matters rested for a while, but then people began to push the story further back. Orthodox mechanistic science had been describing a godless machine-universe, with no final causes (that is, no inbuilt purposiveness and no benevolent Providence), not merely since Darwin, and not merely since Newton, but since René Descartes. Furthermore, it was Descartes above all who had rebuilt the world around an original, self-founding human subject who said *Cogito ergo sum* before he ever needed to think about God, and it was Descartes who was the first really major critical thinker, who had proposed a method of enquiry based upon universal doubt and critical testing. He himself had avoided being too explicit on the point, but in retrospect the Death of God was certain after Descartes.

Nor was this all, for Protestant Reformers such as Luther had already been sceptical about traditional catholic philosophy, had been critical of the Roman Church's claims, and had started from the individual. For them, God could be known only by faith, only as Saviour, and only through the man Jesus Christ. But if God can be accessed only through Christ, then when Christ dies God in effect dies, as a Luther hymn says. It is as if during the 36-hour period of darkness between Good Friday afternoon and Easter morning the whole world becomes a dark and derelict wasteland again. Hence 'Tenebrae'.

Thus the Death of God had already become normalized as part of the annual Christian Year, as part of the life of faith and indeed as part of the experience of many, or most, saints and mystics.[66] In any case, had not the slow decay of theistic philosophy begun back in the Middle Ages, either soon after Thomas Aquinas or perhaps even earlier? Today there are still neo-conservative theologians who want to put a stop to this regress: Wait! they say, at least in Augustine the whole system coheres, correctly balanced.[67] Augustine is the one true Doctor (teacher) of the Latin Church. But the regress cannot be halted even at that point, because everyone knows that 'the crisis of representation' – that is, severe doubts about how one can defend the meaningfulness of ordinary descriptive language that has been stretched to breaking-point in the effort to describe a higher world and a God who, by definition, altogether transcends the limits of the human mind – such doubts go all the way back to Plato, and even Isaiah. Orthodoxy says that God is ineffable, and then goes on to eff him anyway! Augustine was aware of that problem, and so were his immediate predecessors, the Cappadocian Fathers of the Greek Church.

When we are back in the Bible, the hunt starts to become interesting, because the Bible is both pre-philosophical and highly ambivalent about God. The Bible freely uses straightforwardly anthropomorphic imagery in speaking of God and in describing human visions of God, while yet it also fiercely denounces images that picture God in the likeness of anything in heaven or on earth. The God of the Bible is both pure light and total darkness, both luminously intelligible and utterly mysterious.

I have recently[68] been suggesting a Death-of-God reading of the entire Bible narrative from the creation of the world to the final triumph of the Divine Kingdom. Let us tell it again.

This time we begin by asking what the great rationalist philosophers of the past – Greeks like Parmenides, Indians like Shankara – what did they seek? They sought the Real: they asked, 'What is there that is supremely and independently real and intelligible and perfect, and therefore will finally satisfy the philosophical mind?' The answer is always given in terms of thoroughgoing monism. There is only the Absolute, the One, all-inclusive, immutable, perfect, self-sufficient and perfectly simple and intelligible.

As soon as this doctrine about what speculative reason seeks has been stated, we run into problems. How can there be anything else 'beside' the One, or any kind of internal differentiation within it? Further, how can language be used to speak of the One, when as we all know every true sentence says that *S is p, and not not-p*? Language always *differentiates*, and cannot be made to speak simply and plainly of an absolute totality beyond all difference.

These very familiar questions and criticisms apply with particular force to Christianity, because the God of Christianity has from early times been credited *both* with all the metaphysical attributes of the eternal One, *and* with the personal attributes of a 'helicopter parent' who hovers over our human history and over each individual human life, superintending and guiding it all in the direction he has planned. In addition the metaphysical God of Christianity somehow manages, without prejudice to his metaphysical attributes, to make a finite human nature his own in Jesus, and to pour himself out over all the world as Spirit – which makes him three in one, and one in three.

It is all too much. There never was and never will be any way of making clear and consistent sense of such a jumble of conflicting ideas. God cannot be *both* the transpersonal, immutable, Absolute Totality *and* a personal providence with whom humans can have dealings.

There is however a possibility of escape. I've argued that the God of the Bible can be read as a continuous process of self-decentring or handing-over that begins in Genesis, chapter 1.

The biblical writers think in a 'heterological' way. For them the human story is not the story of the ascent of man, but the story of God's progressive self-scattering, and self-dispersal.

In the mythic 'beginning' God is everything, but as soon as God creates man and woman it is obvious in the narrative that God is aware of creating a potential rival, one to whom he will eventually hand over (but not just yet). The narrative particularly mentions human self-consciousness, in the form of shame, and the power of autonomous moral judgement which, as the serpent says to Eve, will make humans 'like God, knowing good and evil'.[69]

So Adam and Eve are turned out of Paradise and into their own long and laborious journey through history. To help them on their way God has already given Adam some power over animals that will help him to hunt them and to domesticate them. In addition, our first parents are burdened with the knowledge of their own mortality.

It is thus notable that although Genesis 1—3 is traditionally read as a Fall story, God has already handed over much to our first parents – enough to distance them a little from God and make them in some degree independent.

Thereafter, God continues to appear on earth among humans and in human guise, at least until the end of Exodus. But the story is one of gradual withdrawal. God appears only on the mountain-top, only to Moses, only to very exceptional figures in rather stylized visions. Instead God disappears behind his own formal utterance in the Law, or in the word spoken by a prophet. Finally, God disappears into the deep darkness of the Holy of Holies in the Temple.

In the New Testament God does not appear in person, but instead disappears behind his own self-revelation in Jesus and his own self-scattering as Spirit, the power of language. In principle, at least, this completes the story of God's long and gradual handover of everything to a new human society. God has completely revealed himself by completely communicating himself to humans. He has died in order to set us free.

Thus the Bible is two interwoven stories. In the *heterological* story, God begins solitary and all-powerful and then gradually over the millennia communicates everything that he is to humans. The *autological* story is the story of the ascent of man, the story of how we humans began with nothing, but through our religious striving gradually appropriated more and more to ourselves until at last we became self-conscious, morally autonomous, free humans who are strong enough to confront the chaos-monster and build our own world for ourselves.

Put the two stories together and we see that God really did make us everything that we are. Coming out of our animal background we were at first desperately weak and vulnerable, and we needed the idea of God (or something else very like it) not merely as a protective fiction but as a role-model, something to live up to.

And what is God? I am suggesting that traditional realist ideas of God as Substance can be entirely replaced by the idea of God as love, God as a continuous process of self-decentring, self-communication, self-scattering through which we humans have become what we are. Remember that the past fifty years has been the age of the Big Bang cosmology. We have learnt to see all reality as a slow-motion explosion, as pouring itself out and passing away, as dissemination. We live in a postmodern epoch in which there is nothing absolute, nothing permanent and nothing substantial. There is only a cosmic pouring out and passing away. It may at first glance seem a bleak and even a nihilistic vision of the world, but no: within universal and End-less transience very great beauties and complexities do arise. One can still be rapt. And I am suggesting that we may be able to rethink philosophy of life, religion and ethics on this model. All life is dying life – including the life of God.

I call the pouring-out-and-passing-away model the 'Fountain'. To say Yes to it, and to model your religion, ethics and lifestyle upon it, is to be 'solar'. Solar living is expressivism, it is pure love, and it is to be lost in life.

We now have at least some of the materials and ideas in place for a rewriting of religious thought within the limits of an Empty-radical-humanist view of the world.

14

The End of Historical Faith

In the past many or most people have been sustained in hard times by some form of hope for a better future that has been nourished by religion. Individuals have been led to hope for vindication and personal happiness after death, and within this life they have also hoped that a just providence will eventually bring them through to better times. At the communal level, many people's hopes have been based upon their community's belief that it has been chosen for a special destiny, and will be preserved until that destiny has been achieved. Around hopes of this latter kind great historical myths have developed, many of them derived from and influenced by Jewish national messianism. The most highly developed and influential Grand Narrative cosmology of all was probably St Augustine's *The City of God*, which became the basis of Latin Christianity, and – in a rather qualified form – was still being recycled by Karl Barth within living memory. Offshoots of the same tradition, which goes back to ancient Persia, include Karl Marx's messianism of the proletariat, and the national messianisms of Imperial Britain, of 'America' and of Russia. Even the European Enlightenment, on its most optimistic fringe, produced a Grand Narrative story about historical progress towards universal human liberation which took various forms between William Godwin and the young H. G. Wells: we could be sure, it was believed, that human life would be progressively improved by the spread of enlightenment, banishing superstition; by liberal humanitarian social reform; and by the endless steady future growth of scientific knowledge and technical power.

History, it was believed, will eventually see everything put right: it will vindicate me – or us. This historical confidence may be grounded upon divine promises and divine providence, or upon the 'historicist' idea that there are ascertainable laws of progressive historical development. People felt sure that time was on their side. But however it was grounded, historical faith, as I shall call it, was undoubtedly very important to very many people in the past. Today, we find that we have lost it, and lost it rather abruptly. And this is undoubtedly a great event.

Personal life after death was still the subject of much anxious enquiry after the First World War, and perhaps also until quite recently. Untimely, premature deaths and undeserved sufferings on a large scale make the topic a matter of personal concern to very large numbers of people. But today, when it has recently been reported that a healthy baby born in a reasonably stable and prosperous Western country now has a life expectancy of around one hundred years, the whole subject is less urgent. We have a new and biology-based understanding of human nature, and of the complex development and slow decline of the human self through the many and various stages of the human life-cycle. So, whereas in the past it was only too easy to yearn after a young person who died young and remains young in death, today it is harder to wish for or to imagine the life after death of someone who has died in extreme old age and after a lengthy decline. Recently I have noticed a new expression coming into use: 'He's had his life.' It implies that our existence has a natural term and that in social conditions where most people, with only a little luck, can expect to have their fair share of life, there is no longer quite the former reason to wish for more. As for the unlucky who die young, today we seem unable to promise more than that we will 'always remember' them.

More generally, critical thinking has made our outlook purely secular, or naturalistic and this-worldly. We simply do not have in our cosmology anywhere to locate the dead and their continuing influence, except in our individual and our corporate memories. There, it is right that we should preserve them.

Our second loss is the loss of all the old Grand Narratives that promised to the nation, or to the community of believers, a blessed future consummation of their history. Only very recently, in the so-called 'noughties' since 2001, have we realized the scale of our loss here. After the sudden collapse of communist party rule in Eastern Europe and the end of the Cold War in 1989–90, there was a brief flowering of American messianism. The United States would collect a very large 'peace dividend', with liberal democracy triumphing worldwide, and US hegemony being unchallenged. History had come to an end (in Hegel's sense of that phrase) with the universal triumph of 'freedom'. Or so it seemed, for a while.

This is not the place to discuss the relative political and economic destabilization of the world since that brief period of optimism. The bigger issues that we must mention are two. First, sudden advances in cheap worldwide mass communications have created a common world-consciousness to a much higher degree than has ever previously existed. Here we are thinking of the completion in the early 1980s of the ring of communications satellites around the globe, and of the extent to which, in conjunction with modern computers and the Internet, satellites and fibre-optic cables are creating not only a single world economy but also a single world conversation of humanity. By itself this development has instantly superseded all merely local ideologies and narratives, political and religious, making them look like fundamentalisms or 'bubbles' that a few inadequates still need to inhabit in order to feel secure.

Still greater, though, is our new general awareness of a really major threat to the collective human future, namely the fact – as it now seems to be – that our present science-based industrial culture, and a human population rising during the present half-century from 6 to 9 billions, are not going to be physically sustainable. Catastrophic climate change is already under way and perhaps cannot now be averted, because the world economic and industrial system is like a vast super-tanker that cannot be turned around in the very few decades we have left. In the major Western economies political and economic decline has already begun – for example in Britain and California – so that society is already fast losing the strength to finance and to execute the very large-scale capital projects needed to secure the supplies of electricity, fresh water and food, and the flood defences that will fend off social breakdown. Americans in particular are traditionally very good at science, very good at changing fast, very good at industry, and very good at organization. They if anyone should be capable of responding appropriately. But now in California the state is bankrupt, and life goes on as usual: they are still watering their golf courses, turning up the air-conditioning, and filling their swimming pools. Clearly, there is no chance that they will wake up until it is much too late; and a fortiori, what is true of them is likely to prove true of the rest of humanity. We'll do too little, too late.

Suddenly, all the older and more optimistic religions and political visions of the future have shrivelled. A very large crow has appeared and it makes the squabbles of Tweedledum and Tweedledee in the Middle East, for example, seem irrelevant. The best we can hope for and work for is sustainability. In the short run, failed states, much suffering and forced population reduction have already begun in some countries, and there will be much more of the same to come. Some biologist friends tell me that there have been half-a-dozen mass-extinction events before, but life has gone on.[70] This time we may extinguish ourselves, but they are content to think that at least *their* subject-matter will continue in being and take new forms. As for the arts subjects, the humanities, they will all be turned into one great super-subject: archaeology.

Historical faith, as we said we'd call it, is coming to an end. But we may be able to preserve a little of the best of our cultural tradition: science, music, philosophy, Buddhist spirituality, Christian culture, cheap information technology. Perhaps we can learn to live without constant 'growth', and the use of mechanized transport? Perhaps: but the transition, even if we can make it successfully, will be extremely painful.

Most difficult of all will be the task of learning to renounce the principal motor of historical change hitherto, namely male aggression, male competition and male struggles for power, leadership, domination. Karl Marx saw the extent to which struggle, and in particular *class* struggle, has been the motor of history, and Michel Foucault has recently made us more aware of 'micropower' – the struggle for dominance in all human relationships.[71] But it is not easy for us to grasp how deep is the connection between *historical faith* and (principally male) contestation for power.

Here is a small illustration of the point. Suppose you are a man who has arranged to meet again another man – maybe a former student or neighbour – whom you knew quite well for a while thirty, forty or even fifty years ago. How will you recognize him, after so many years? What is the one characteristic that you will never forget, and that will not have changed? Answer, his *height*. When one man meets another the first thing he notices is their relative heights, and he never forgets it – so deeply engrained is the competitiveness of men.

Now this competitiveness of men is fundamental to historical faith, whether religious or political. Every 'historical' theology or political ideology claims to know that things soon can be, will be, are sure to be better. But Rome wasn't built in a day, and the Better World is still some distance away. To reach it, we need to stick together during our long march through history. In fact, we need organization, we need discipline, we need *leadership*. Thus, Jesus' radically egalitarian message about the divine Kingdom evolved quickly into Apostolic government of the Church, and Marx's message about the communist society quickly developed into Marxism-Leninism-Stalinism and the dictatorship of the proletariat; and in our own time Señor Chavez assures people that in order to build true socialism in Venezuela it is necessary that the country's constitution be amended so that he personally can become President for Life. Nobody laughs. Historical faith always sustains a community's march through time, and to keep order on the march there must be an officer class, there must be hierarchy, there must be *rule* – and therefore there must be competition (almost entirely among males) for positions of leadership. My own church is kept on the road and believing the faith entirely by the loud protestations of their own orthodox faith that come from all the well-groomed and 'focused' young priests who are competing for future leadership.

Thus if in the future we must learn to live sustainably, without all the traditional ideas of growth and progressive development, there will have to be enormous changes in our psychological make-up and in our institutions. Very roughly, we need to become more Buddhist in outlook. All 'narrative systematics' – that is, stories about the community's long march through history towards a promised Better World – will have to go. We don't want either the supernaturalism, or the long-termism, or the cosmic Grand Narrative doctrinal systems. Nor do we want or need the discipline and the hierarchically governed community that go with historical faith. Instead, our religion will be a collection of personal religious skills and habits, which we will acquire by criticizing our values, by training our attention and our feelings, and by learning how to live our own transient lives.[72]

15

In Passing

The verb 'to pass' is one of the most beautiful in the language. It comes from the Latin *passus*, a pace, so that to pass is originally simply *to walk by* something. Around this core a wide range of metaphorical extensions of the word have developed: words *pass one's lips*, something that is just about adequate *passes muster*, by *passing an examination* one moves up a grade (*gradus*, a step), and at the end of their lives people *pass away*.

Time also passes. We speak of *the passing show of existence*, and in the most beautiful idiom of them all say of any happening that *it comes to pass*.

Everything comes into being and passes away. Everything is transient (going across, Latin *transire*; hence also transitory, in transit, transition).

Evidently we have here a cluster of ideas that are deeply embedded in our language, and indeed have been accepted general truths of the human condition as it has been understood, both in the Hebrew/Greek and in the Indian cultural traditions, and both in religion and in philosophy, ever since they first began. In the world around us, the human lifeworld, everything is contingent, everything is temporal and transient. Everything comes to be and passes away. I like to put the point by writing Being or existence as a participle, be-ing. All be-ing is subject to time: everything comes and goes – including you and me.

At this point there is likely to be a sudden change of tone, because many – perhaps even *most* – people are apt to find the thought of universal contingency and transience terrifying when they belatedly grasp that it really does apply to themselves and to everything they value. At present they are immersed in life, their environment, their various interests and responsibilities; and their diaries are crowded and busy – and now they suddenly understand that before long they must *come to nothing*; just cease to exist. They are incredulous and angry: they are too busy to die, they haven't time for death.

At this point, the argument changes direction. We began by thinking it an easy, obvious, universal truth that everything is contingent and everything passes away. Now we begin trying to claim that when they are thought through, all the way, the generalizations are after all not fully coherent. If everything is contingent and transient and nothing is necessary and eternal, there might at any moment suddenly be nothing at all. Surely, the general truth that everything is contingent is consistently thinkable only against the background of there being something eternal and necessary in which it is grounded, and from which it proceeds? Rather as the beam of light coming from a cinema projector needs to fall upon an unmoving screen in order to *show up*, so the ever-changing contingent world of phenomena needs an unchanging background against which it can *show up* and be understood.

Metaphysics, and philosophical theism in particular, often begins from here. Temporality, thought through, is seen to need the idea of something eternal that abides in the background. Contingency seems to need the thought of something necessary in the background, something that *frames* the passing show of existence, *underlies* it, and *endures*. Something that holds everything together and makes it all intelligible.

In this way the thought of God or the Absolute, and with it the thought perhaps of personal immortality for ourselves, and the thought of eternal norms of intelligibility and value, begins to seem very attractive. But there are no two doubts. First, there is that little hiccup at the beginning when we first said: 'Everything is fleeting'; but wait, that thought cannot itself quite be carried through. Can there be thought without any objective anchorage at all? If *everything* is slippery, there's no foothold. So we must amend the doctrine, and say: 'Everything is transient'; therefore there must be some deep and dark unchanging background Reality that grounds the flux of appearances, and enables them to show up.

Alternatively, we may simply say: 'Is the doctrine that "everything changes" *itself* an eternal truth, or is it itself only contingently true, just for now?', and so see the loophole as arising through that paradox. Thus, similarly, if the doctrine that everything is relative is itself only relativistically true, a vortex suddenly opens, and the mind goes spinning down. Which is taken to show that thought is not possible without fixed points of some kind. And, of course, my own impending death makes my head spin in that same way, because it's so hard clearly to think one's own non-existence. 'All men are mortal' is easy: 'I must soon die' is difficult to handle, especially when at last it's true.

So much for the first hiccup. But the second is equally serious and disorienting. Suppose that, impressed by the foregoing considerations, we embrace some version of Platonic philosophy. Beyond this world of changing appearances there is an eternal world, a better world, a higher world. If we keep an eye on that world of eternal truths and standards we will be able to orient ourselves and walk tall in this life. We are on a long journey towards our true and eternal home in the world above. Ideally, if we get our priorities right, we should spend the whole of this relatively wretched life here below in rational contemplation of eternity. All truth, all value, all happiness are to be found only in the world above.

That, however, is the second hiccup: for if Platonism is really true we should despise this world and its delights, because they are vain. We should live the life of reason, and become contemplative monks and nuns. But since the Middle Ages there has been a turn of human attention towards this world and this life, and on a very large scale. The colossal growth of natural science and of historical knowledge, together with an entirely new understanding of our own biological background and make-up, and a new philosophy of language – all this has completely embedded us in this life, this human life-world. Nietzsche's indignation against a philosophical and religious tradition that alienated men and women from themselves and from the only life we will ever have seems entirely justified. From now on, any tolerable future ethic, or philosophy of life, or faith must be purely naturalistic or this-worldly in outlook.

Very well, but can our new naturalism of the human life-world – 'this life is all there is'– can it endure the thought of the pure contingency and the possibilities of utter disaster that always threaten it, and the ultimate Nothingness or emptiness that always surrounds it and into which we must all of us pass? We may whistle to keep our spirits up, but deep down do we not have the horrors, all the time? Is it not true that our own future decline and death tend to become the great Unmentionables?

Atheistic humanists, following Nietzsche, will remind us at this point that the end of repressive, life-denying religion is, and should be experienced as, a great blessing. All the value that was sucked out of life by Platonism and monasticism is now free to return into life. And why should we not learn to die exactly as a person falls asleep at the end of a long and busy day? Why not?

Further, it is added that nostalgia for what we have lost is misplaced. When we fully recognize how completely we are always immersed in temporality, we will see how utterly impossible it is to imagine human personal life *except* in time, in language, in the body, and so on. We cannot consistently think through the claim that in another world the conditions of our life might be radically different from what they are. So we should simply dismiss false regrets and say Yes to life as it is. We'll never know anything else.

All that is true, but in this book I am arguing that there is more to be said. It is true that some kind of secular-humanist outlook is inescapable today. My version of the doctrine is 'Empty radical humanism'. But remember that according to both the Hebrew Bible *and* the New Testament human beings were originally created just for life on this earth, and the final consummation of our religion will *also* be realized on this earth. To put it crudely, 'secular' means 'of this present world, or this present era', and secular humanism is a human-centred and purely this-worldly outlook. But according to the Bible Adam and Eve in paradise were secular humanists, God becoming man in Christ accepts secular humanity and its fate as his own, and the Kingdom of God on earth is a blessed future state of human *secular* existence.

Thus the religious outlook of the Bible is much more secular and humanistic than many people realize. Because after his death Jesus did *not* return at once to establish his Kingdom on earth, the Church developed to fill the period of waiting for his return – and the Church certainly *is* Platonic and other-worldly, indeed. It looks up to heaven while the Lord is still there. But the Church is only a temporary institution, a stopgap. Today, when ecclesiastical other-worldliness is passing away, it is not at all surprising that a good deal of the old religion is returning to us in new and strange guises. And if in our new secular humanism there still lurks a certain repressed fear and horror, then perhaps it needs to be and can be cured by religion as it too returns into secularity. If that is so, then *even within a secular-humanist world-view*, Christianity may still be able to function as a religion of redemption.

In this context, what does theology's strange return look like? We have seen a return of the old theology going on for some centuries now, in the first appearance and then the gradual spread of *extravertive mysticism*. This is a mysticism of this world and of the sense of sight. Things look brilliantly coloured, super-real, throbbing with significance. In the poets (Henry Vaughan, Thomas Traherne and William Wordsworth) this vision of the world is associated especially with early childhood, but in painting – perhaps especially in Samuel Palmer's Shoreham works,[73] in French Impressionism and post-Impressionism, and above all in Vincent Van Gogh – the extravertive mystic's vision of the world is very well and effectively democratized. (In passing, it's worth remarking that photography is perhaps the most democratic of the visual arts, and that photography too finds eternal significance in the fleeting moment.) As we commented earlier in connection with Wordsworth, in this kind of mysticism divine glory is no longer strictly an attribute of God: it has become diffused over the whole world of our visual experience. God has been decentred, made ubiquitous.

How has extravertive mysticism, which first appeared among a very small elite at the tail end of the Middle Ages, been able to spread so widely that today something of it is familiar to nearly everyone – for example, through cinema? Wordsworth attributes the whole thing to the greatness of the human mind;[74] but I do not quite agree. Rather, it is the decline of dogmatism that has gradually 'cleansed the doors of perception', enabling us to look at everything with a more innocent eye. Vastly improved scientific knowledge and optical instruments have taught us to see much more, and our late Modern recognition of the utter gratuitousness of all existence enables us to see everything as a wonderful gift. For me the sky, insects, green grass in strong sunshine, wildfowl in flight, limestone landscapes: and for you, what? As I see it, the crucial point is that the decline of Platonism and dogmatic faith has been a huge religious gain, because it has allowed religious and aesthetic value to flood back into the world of ordinary sensuous experience. Losing the old kind of faith really has been gain. Life has become beautiful: we have recovered at least something of what Nietzsche calls 'the innocence of becoming'.

Something similar is to be said about the modern recovery of the old sacred power of language. In dogmatic religion of the ecclesiastical kind, religious language undergoes a steady decline. It slowly turns into a series of stock slogans that are used as passwords in order to demonstrate one's own loyal membership of the group and to check other people's credentials. Eventually these slogans become so meaningless and irritating as to be quite unusable by anyone who cares about language. Happily, with the Romantic Movement there began to develop in the West a much superior philosophy of language in both the Anglo-Saxon and the Continental traditions. This opens up the possibility of a new age in which we may be able completely to abandon religious dogma and dogmatic orthodoxy, and replace it by the habit of using poetical language to establish and to communicate a religious vision of life. Much of the vocabulary will doubtless continue to be Christian – I'll be glad if it does – but we will completely abandon the hideous old obsession with using Christian vocabulary to police the frontiers of the community, to divide *us* from *them*, and to confirm hierarchies of spiritual power.

In this chapter we have discussed two aspects of theology's strange return within the secular-humanist world-view of the period since around 1790. They are the return of divine glory in the glowing brightness of the world of our visual experience, and the return of the old sacred power of language since the Romantic Movement. These two topics underlay the discussions in Chapters 1–6, 9, 11 and 12, and they are intimately linked. It is after all *language*, and not only the language of poetry but also the language of modern science and modern critical history, which has differentiated and theorized the world and thereby has hugely enriched our visual experience.

Imagine two people walking together in the country. One of them has read his historical geography, his Hoskins, his Rackham, and the rest,[75] and can *read* the ages of stone walls and hedges, the shapes of fields and farmsteads, and the history of the whole landscape. He takes it for granted for one should be able to identify the trees, the birds, the insects, the soil types and the rocks. The other knows and cares nothing about any of these topics, but merely enjoys the walk. Which of the two has the better vision: which of the two can better *tell* what he's looking at? Whose world is *brighter*?

In future, we should see an obvious alliance and connection between education, the brightening of sense-experience, and the development of a religious vision of life. So far, we've only just begun to recover from a curious neglect, even *poisoning*, of the sense of sight that lasted for some thirteen centuries. St Bernard of Clairvaux, for example, a great saint, shut his eyes to pray, loved spiritual power, blind as a bat. And Protestant-ism, for the most part, was even *worse*.

16

Man Made God Made Man

What in the end is the big difference between the species *Homo sapiens* and the other surviving great apes to whom we are most closely allied? During the past half-century the labours of primatologists and psychologists have put a question mark against almost all traditional answers to this question. A famous experiment with a dot of paint and a mirror appears to show that chimpanzees and orang-utans are self-aware. Chimpanzees, and a few other primates, are capable of tool-using, of manipulating quite a large vocabulary of symbols, of problem-solving, of transmitting successful behaviours socially as if they were traditions, and of many other skills. The line between man and other animals seems to be getting more and more blurred. Yet there surely is still an enormous difference between a chimpanzee and an undergraduate. What is it? How, without any significant change in our basic biology, have we managed to come so far, so quickly?

It is that humans alone have over the millennia evolved a large and complex ideal culture, a world of ideas which every member of a human society carries around in his or her head. By these ideas they live. During most of the Palaeolithic period, when we were slowly emerging from our animal background, human intelligence was still only 'modular'; that is, we had developed valuable survival skills in a few areas such as social relationships, tool- and weapon-making, and knowledge of animals and edible plants. But that was about all we had.[76] The human mind was not yet unified, and its counterpart, our cosmology or general world-view, was not yet unified either. Our level of self-awareness was rather low. Both

in the world and within the self we perceived only a scrim-
mage of violent non-rational forces. It was a bit like being
stuck in a bad dream: one did not fully *grasp* either oneself,
or one's world, or what was happening to one – dreams being
of course a useful relic of archaic forms of consciousness to
which all of us have ready access.

We desperately needed ideal culture in order to get hold
of ourselves and our world. This ideal culture must give us a
spatiotemporal framework within which to operate (ideas of
territory, and of an annual cycle), and persuade us that within
that framework we can project out around ourselves an ordered regular life-world that we can learn to understand and
control. Ideal culture must also make us more self-aware and
self-disciplined, and able to understand the feelings and guess
the intentions of others. It must convince us that it is possible
for us so to 'transcend' our own lower natures that we can
plan and execute projects, and frame a life for ourselves with
others, in a social world and in accordance with rational and
moral principles. Evidentially our ideal culture must also give
us core ethical ideas of free will, and obedience to standard
moral principles that bind everyone. And when we have got
this far, it is clear that we have left our primate relatives far
behind. We have become human.

There's a snag. The whole arduous process of cultural development from animal to human depends upon the very first
step: getting human consciousness unified and 'centred'. We
needed somehow to be able to pull ourselves up out of the
raw violence of animal feeling, and to become conscious of
ourselves. We needed a bit of self-transcendence. We needed
to get above ourselves in order to take charge of ourselves.
Reason must learn to govern the emotions, exactly as a man
trains and learns to ride a horse. But in this case we need a
jump to a higher level, an act of transcendence, so that we can
get a grip of ourselves and learn to control ourselves and our
world. How can we do this? We need somehow to make and
enforce a very clear distinction between flesh and spirit, the
passions and reason, horse and rider, our lower nature and

our true and 'higher' selves. But how was all this to be done? Remember: at this very early stage we did not know, and *could* not know, what we needed.

It was done, not by introducing a certain duality into *our-selves*, for that was impossibly difficult, but by splitting objective reality. Those mysterious fearsome impersonal forces and powers outside ourselves, which together were all we originally knew of the world, were split in two. There was the particular region or phenomenon, and there was the sacred, numinous spirit-power that 'haunted' that particular place. Thus the emergent world was divided into two zones: Nature, and the spirit-world that haunted and controlled it, the visible world and its many invisible controlling sacred Powers, earth and heaven, natural and supernatural. There is a relic of this origin of the spirit-world in classical literature, in such phrases as the 'genius loci', the spirit of a place, the 'numen' that haunted some particular grove, mountain, river, cave or tree.

Thus all speculative thought was at first *heterological*. We couldn't possibly have introduced the flesh/spirit distinction directly into our own weak and patchy selves. Instead, we introduced it into our environment. Now theology really did become the mother and queen of all sciences, for humans could make progress from now on by learning how to deal with the spirits. In order to deal with them we had to develop a language – ritual – and thus to get clearer about what the spirits are, what powers they have, how we can please them and so on. And, as Hegel said of the Master–Servant relationship generally, the Servant who really *studies* his Master gradually becomes like his master; gradually learns that he himself is the one who in the end does all the work and has all the power. So, at this very early stage, we learnt how to become free, conscious selves who could understand and control our environment by first postulating, and then dealing with, copying and learning from beings who had the powers we lacked. It was a roundabout procedure: I call it 'heterological', but the more usual term is 'mythical thinking'.

As the history of religion then continues, theology, anthropology and cosmology develop in parallel, and reflect each other. But we are talking about religion, and about human spiritual development along a heterological track; so theology has to be in the lead. The spirits grow in power, and eventually settle down when men do, to become gods. Then the gods get themselves organized into a pantheon, under the presidency of a supreme god, a sky-father, king and legislator. Now the pantheon is the heavenly counterpart of the city-state on earth. The gods are organized into a society, each god having a social function. Correspondingly, the cosmos is becoming more unified and law-governed, and the human self too is slowly becoming unified. But the old plurality of the self survived until surprisingly late. The ancient Egyptians, having a notoriously large number of gods, had in themselves seven souls, whose gradual coming apart at death was splendidly described in 150 pages by the underestimated American writer Norman Mailer.[77] The literary form of *allegory* reflects a plurality within the human self which was deeply felt in Latin antiquity and continued in use by poets almost till modern times.[78]

So the unification of the spirit-world into fully developed ethical monotheism wasn't really completed until the end of what we commonly think of as 'the Old Testament period'. It was still being completed in Jesus' time. The unification of the cosmos into a single law-governed universe was envisaged by Aristotle, but not really completed until Galileo. And the moral unification of the sovereign, rational, free, individual human self, though envisaged by the philosophers (*and by Jesus himself*[79]) quite early, was not fully completed until Latin Europe's second 'Enlightenment', in the eighteenth century. It has been a very long, hard struggle; and to this day there are still a very large number of human beings who do not wish to become fully adult. They prefer 'fundamentalism'.

Why fundamentalism? Remember, God has a biography too, which exactly parallels ours and all along has guided us through our own spiritual development. God's job was gradually to show us how to create and order our world, how to be a rational and autonomously legislating individual, how to set out and execute a great and good purpose, how to search other people's hearts and know what they are thinking, and so on. But when God himself came of age in fully developed monotheism, it was not hard for a religiously gifted individual to see that as man follows him and *also* comes of age, there must be conflict between them, and the number of solutions is limited. Either God must progressively hand over everything to man and himself retreat into obscurity or die; or alternatively, God must himself actually *become* man. Perhaps the second of these solutions is in Christianity a hyperbolic version of the first. And we haven't yet mentioned a third possible solution, found recently in our Western postmodernity: both God *and* man must be decentred and disappear into the endless glittering motion of language. This last solution, by bringing the West and the middle-way Buddhist East together, gives some promise of offering a possible fully globalized religious future. But it makes the preceding story even stranger: we toiled for tens of thousands of years to develop the ideas of a supernatural world, and eventually of ethical monotheism. Then we toiled for almost two thousand years in order to become free and fully adult human selves. Then within two hundred years comes the Death of Man. Today we could be facing the final destruction of our whole cultural tradition by runaway climate change, within around a hundred years. Very rum: a grandiose tragedy, but on the worst-case scenario there will be no audience for it. We'll leave only archaeology, but even if a much-reduced human community survives, nobody will have much inclination to dig us up.

17

Ourselves, God's Legacy

In the previous chapter we discussed ways in which God may return, and may continue to be seen as our maker, even within a purely secular-humanist world-view. Since the human self was originally forged in and by its relation to God, people have grown to be like their own ethnic gods, and even after having become completely secular a person may still bear the image of the God in whom his or her ancestors once believed.

To spell all this out in more detail, in the Palaeolithic period there was no way of dragging a lazy and confused ape out of his immersion in raw Nature and giving him more self-knowledge and better control of his environment (*Weltherrschaft*, 'world-mastery' as the Germans used to call it), other than by splitting his surrounding Other into two levels: the natural world, and a world of spirits that inhabited, haunted and controlled it. This was the very beginning of the distinctions between natural and supernatural, the world and God, body and mind, and the passions and reason. In each case something 'higher', invisible and very active is seen as presiding over, and perhaps *animating* something lower, visible and relatively blind or inert.

To return: once a distinction of this kind has been made, early humans have the task of learning how to deal with the spirits, how to communicate with them, how to understand what they are, and how they control events. Theology becomes humankind's chief intellectual pursuit, and it will yield as by-products two great and growing constructs: the world and the self. Even to this day in Western metaphysics and in modern philosophy the self and the world still run parallel and reflect each other: microcosm and macrocosm, the little world of the self and the big world that is the cosmos.

As theology develops, and conceptions of what spirits are, how they function, and what they require of us become clearer, we gradually become more like the spirit-beings in whom we believe. Around the world, ancient spirituality always directs the believer to set aside or to put down the lower, more emotional and animal side of his own make-up, and instead to concentrate on developing his more spirit-like capacities: reason, self-criticism, flights of thought, sustained attention. Gradually the spirits develop into local gods, and then into a pantheon. With the development of a centred city-state, the gods can settle down into fixed, permanent habitations of their own. They sit enthroned. They get themselves organized into a pantheon under the presidency of a supreme sky-father, and share out the principal tasks – war, agriculture, technology, lawgiving etc. – among themselves. In effect, the gods come to form a heavenly counterpart to the state down below on earth, and the development towards absolute monarchy over a great empire below on earth parallels the development towards absolute ethical monotheism in the heavenly world above. In Imperial Russia, for example, God was the Great Father, and the Tsar was the Little Father.

As all this happens, the emergent One God hauls us humans along with himself, so that we can still be lesser counterparts of himself. Like him we can learn to project out an orderly, intelligible world around ourselves, laying down its Law, and making it a realm in which we ourselves, like God, can plan and implement a great moral purpose. The idea that when we build our natural philosophy we learn 'to think God's thoughts after him', profoundly influenced the rise of early modern physics in the seventeenth-century West between Galileo and Newton, so close to each other are the ideas of God and the self. Our science actually arose in the Cartesian belief that we can know the world as God knows it. The same principle holds in the ethical realm: we first imagined

God as *covenanting* himself to his creation, pledging himself to uphold its order, and then as *covenanting* himself ethically to his chosen people; and only *then* did we become capable of developing and theorizing all the *human* ethical ideas of vowing, contracting, promising, undertaking, covenanting and pledging. Indeed, God demands of us mimesis, reciprocity, copying of his ethical nature. He had himself become ethical, and now he taught us ethics.

So it goes on: modern secular people, laying down the law, building their worlds, doing their science and technology, and also signing their contracts and making promises, are still recognizably the children of the God in whom their ancestors believed. So God returns indirectly and reminds us of himself even within a culture that has been secular-humanist since the rise of the modern novel over two centuries ago. We still have the old God's thumbprints all over us. Long, long ago, through the slow evolution of ancient theology, we made spirits, and finally God, in the image of what we obscurely knew we wanted to become; *and it worked*, as God then re-made us in his own image, and gave us something of his own world-mastery. Now, long afterwards, after the Death of God we ourselves are God's legacy, his testament. What we are makes his absence conspicuous, for we are still evidently his children. Just as ex-Catholics are still evidently Catholics, so modern post-theists are still in a sense theists. For example, the popular Oxford controversialist and Darwinian Richard Dawkins is still very theistic in his confidence that there is a law-governed intelligible world out there that he can know because his mind too works in rules, in a way that parallels the world-order. He is confident in the clarity of his own rationality, and in the notion of a pre-established harmony between the order of our thinking and the world-order. So he remains profoundly a child of God, and I hope he's pleased to hear it. He should be.

To develop the point further, the history of religion is always also the history of the human self, all the way up from the stage at which the self was nothing more than a dark turmoil of conflicting feelings and forces with only an occasional flash of illumination here and there, to the appearance now after the Enlightenment, after Kant and after Nietzsche of fully 'adult' modern humans. It has been a long, hard journey. If we reflect upon it we will understand why the care of the self (Foucault's *pratique de soi*) has played such a large part in the practice of religion. Religion's task was to develop the self: self-examination, the struggle for self-mastery and self-purification, disciplines of prayer and meditation, rules of life – all these were pursued until 'spirituality' (or inwardness, or subjectivity) became the creation of an inner monastery with many chambers inside the self, the so-called 'interior castle'. The typical religious act was the act of recollecting oneself into one's own subjectivity, turning inwards.

Today, the best way to explain the postmodern decentring of the self is to see it as telling us that inwardness or subjectivity has come to the end of its usefulness. If you pursue inwardness too determinedly today, you will end up in black psychotic depression. There are all too many admonitory examples of very good people to whom it has recently happened. The moral is that the interior castle was only ever a human cultural construct. Once it did a useful job, but now we should abandon it. Don't cling to your own inner life any longer: forget it, and pour yourself out over the whole world, as God has done. Stop being introvertive and intropunitive, and start being extravertive. Start seeing the visual field as the field of consciousness, and pour yourself out into the world. Be *solar*, like God, again, for God has no inner life at all. He is self-decentring by nature. He pours himself out like the sun, all the time, passing away. Thus the highest development of the idea of God coincides with the highest development of the self. The Death of God and the Death of Man still run in parallel, and the life of love is still a dying life for both of us, for him and for me.

Throughout the model as I have described it runs the assumption that normally God and the human self evolve in step, with God only a little way ahead of the self, for the obvious reason that we could imagine a spirit only a little more unified and with only a little more self-knowledge, world-mastery and moral goodness than we ourselves had attained or could imagine. So God needs to be ahead of us to be aspired after, but can only be a little ahead of us.

There is an obvious and important exception to this general rule. Israel (literally: 'the one who strives with God') seems to have produced a number of figures who had got somewhat ahead of God, and for this reason were in a position to challenge God, and even to worst him in argument. Nietzsche took it that Abraham had been such a figure, and therefore supposed that he (Abraham) and someone like Odysseus in the Greek tradition had been on the point of becoming fully modern post-Death-of-God humans three millennia ago. I am not sure of the timing at this point, because the dating of Genesis that was beginning to be accepted in Nietzsche's time now looks very doubtful. But it *is* true that the Israelite tradition *dramatizes* the man–God relation very powerfully, and in clear awareness of the possibility that a human being may be smarter than God, and may therefore outgrow his God. Notoriously, the cleverest Jews have a very high level of ironical self-awareness, whereas God – especially in the earlier books of the Old Testament – had a strikingly *low* level of self-awareness, so that the comic possibilities of the God–man relationship are obvious.

However, the single most important case of all this is the case of the blasphemer, heretic and would-be destroyer of the Law, Jesus of Nazareth.[80] The reason why Jesus got into such severe trouble was that he tried to bring into the present a construction of the world, of God and of the self that belonged to a still-remote future. He was much too far ahead of his time, and suffered accordingly.

Jesus appears to have been influenced by the visions of the future of God and of the self that are to be found in the prophetic writings. In the early synagogue-Judaism that Jesus knew, God had already become a remote Sovereign, whose relation to man was mediated by a written Law-code, the

Torah. He had long since ceased to appear in person. God was Writing, God was the Law, religion was pious study of canonical texts. The prophets Jeremiah, Ezekiel and others had long ago – as it seemed – declared that this kind of mediated religion must in the long run fail. Strict observance of religious Law was not a sufficient basis for either religion or social ethics, and the prophets looked forward to a better future in which religion and morality would become altogether more spontaneous and immediate. People needed new 'hearts': religion needed to be internalized. God would write his law upon their hearts, God would take away their hearts of stone and give them hearts of flesh, God would put his Spirit into their hearts.[81]

What is 'the heart', here? Intentions, or feelings? Feelings, I think, as is suggested by the contrast between the stony heart and a heart of flesh that has melted. At any rate Jesus' own ethical teaching is best seen as radicalizing and real-izing this strand of accepted prophetic teaching. When he talks about the Kingdom of God, he is impatiently attempting to bring a dreamt-of future world into the present. In that future world God will be decentred, distributed into humans, 'poured out upon all flesh'. Jesus had an exceptionally strong ethical vision, and for him the most important thing of all was the relationship between one human being and the next. He wanted an ethics of love, and his view of ethics was emotivist and expressivist. Good and evil are of the heart, and in the end are determined *only* by the human heart.[82] Human beings are the only possible inventors of ethics.

In a word, what Jesus meant by the Kingdom of God was what we mean by the Death of God: God decentred, dispersed into individuals as in left Quakerism, and the human self similarly solar, generous, self-outpouring, living by dying, passing away. No wonder he was executed: the authorities could hardly do anything else with such a spectacular anachronism. He was a young man in too much of a hurry.

And what were his small band of surviving followers to do without him? They had little choice but to compromise

94

with history, and develop a religion halfway between the social reality of their own period and the almost-postmodern radical-humanist utopia of love that Jesus had envisaged. About twenty years after his death they began to speak of him as risen and exalted to heaven, where he was enthroned at God's right hand until the time was ripe for his return to establish his Kingdom on earth. In Christian art the upshot of this was the standard image of Christ Almighty, King of the Universe, sitting enthroned on a rainbow, or on the firmament. His iconography – the robes, the nimbus and so on – was that of the Emperor. So the image was a radical-humanist image: in Jesus, an historical man is on the throne of the universe. The entire cosmos is just the human life-world. The *only* world is the human world: Christianity *is* humanism. But at the same time, the Church keeps God the Father as a shadow in the background. God is still rigorously aniconic and Jesus is his only human face, the only image of him that is tolerated. It is a clever compromise and it worked pretty well until about the fourteenth century, when some people in the West began to give God the Father a distinct human image of his own – inevitably, that of an old man, like the apostle Paul. This causes trouble, for by the time of Hubert and Jan Van Eyck's Ghent Altarpiece of 1432, people are becoming somewhat unsure about the identity of the grave, bearded cosmic Monarch who presides over a major work of religious art: is this God the Father, or is it Christ Almighty? Both are human: they look rather alike; which is which?

In the case of the Ghent Altarpiece, *The Adoration of the Lamb*, the ambiguity is especially acute. The presiding central figure is surely and rightly Christ in Majesty, flanked by figures of the Virgin Mary and of John the Baptist, who is pointing to him as usual. But, very significantly, this Christ has appropriated to himself some of the iconography of God the Father.[83] In particular, he wears the papal tiara. Now usually in fifteenth- and sixteenth-century art Christ is identified with the Emperor and wears a crown, marking his subordination in obedience to God the Father, who is identified with the

Pope and wears the tiara. Remember: Latin Christian art is about power – and in particular about the power-struggle between Church and State. Images of the Trinity often make the point clearly. But the Van Eyck Christ wears the papal tiara, and *not* the crown, which is on the floor at his feet. Further down the midline of the polyptych, the Dove descends upon the Lamb to complete a standard image of the Trinity with, again, Christ in the seat of God the Father.

Some of the inscriptions point the same way: the texts on the moulded arches around the head of Christ are not christological, but just refer to God generally. On his robe is visible the word SABAOTH (Hebrew: 'of the heavenly hosts') from the ancient Israelite title of God, 'Lord of Hosts'.

All this does suggest something we often feel in connection with fifteenth-century painting in the Low Countries and down the Rhine: namely that, consciously or not, late medieval art was teetering on the brink of a breakthrough to Christian radical humanism.

18

The Proper Study of Humankind

Philosophical thought – and religious thought too, perhaps, nowadays – very often begins with wonder; wonder at existence in general, and at human existence in particular. The very way people phrase their questions about existence commonly betrays the influence of various older visions of the world. *Why are we here?* they ask, inviting the retort: 'What makes you think there ought to be a *reason* for our existence, waiting to be found?' *What are we here for?* they ask, this time inviting the retort: 'What makes you so keen to hear that we have all been chosen to fulfil some great superhuman cosmic purpose?' There are after all about 6.5 billion of us, living in almost 200 sovereign nation-states. Can we all of us have predestined roles in a single great drama with an ultimately highly edifying plot?

The traditional great questions of life seem very often to be either clichés, or too vaguely phrased, or born of over-optimistic expectations.[84] In the discussion so far I have proposed two principal factors in the making of humankind. First: language, in the sense of simple forms of symbolic exchange, may be seen as having begun among our ape-like ancestors. It produced the very beginnings of inter-subjectivity and of consciousness. And second, our long struggle for better understanding and control of ourselves and of our environment led to our postulating an unseen world of spirits which had all the freedom and control over nature (not to mention, access to other human hearts) that we needed. By our dealings with the supernatural world and our thought about it we gradually formed and developed all our basic ideas of God, of the world, and of ourselves. In a catch-phrase: *We made God make us.*

To make further progress, we need to consider the great classic metaphors under which people have always seen human life.

Because until only 10–12,000 years ago all human beings were nomads, our life has always been spoken of as a *journey*. There are three main kinds of journey: in *picaresque narrative* the individual is buffeted and blown all over the place by the winds of life, and must survive by his or her guile. The hero experiences extraordinary reversals of fortune, but somehow comes through. He has *lived by his wits*, as the phrase goes. In the *quest*, the individual leaves home searching for some goal that he cannot clearly specify, but confident that he will recognize it when he comes across it. And in the *pilgrimage*, the individual sets out to reach a specified destination, a renowned holy place and goal of life about which she has long been taught.

As for human social life, that too has for about 3,000 years been seen under three great metaphors. Society is seen as a *body* politic, with individuals making each their own contribution to the functioning of the whole, much as its various organs work together in the human body. Alternatively, society may be seen as a *market*, with each person putting out her stall, displaying her wares, and trading with others. We all seek attention: we all have something to trade. And third, society may be seen as a *theatre*. A '*persona*' was originally a role in a play, and in our social relations with other people we are always playing the roles of child, parent, lover, teacher, spouse, worker, employer, friend and so on. Every day, we slip surprisingly easily and quickly from one role to another.

What is the best lifestyle for a human being? Here, two great metaphors compete. The *soldier* is a person content to give his whole life to the service of a great institution. It finds him a place in its ranks, and he is happy to be a faithful servant, who does his duty and obeys orders. He slots himself into place in the job he loves. By contrast, the *artist* is a free spirit who prefers to start from nothing and to make everything up for herself as she goes along. Such a person is very highly inner-directed: something wells up inside her all the time, steering her life, showing her what she must do next. In order to concentrate on listening to that inner wellspring of creativity you really must shut out all other voices and other claims. It's not easy, for a woman-artist.

Finally, we come to the all-important metaphor which has haunted these pages, the metaphor of *imprisonment and escape*, or release or liberation. Here we are thinking of a very long tradition in both philosophy and religion which suggests that ordinary human existence is somehow unsatisfactory. Human life seems to be hedged in by limitations that are very hard or even impossible to escape. The limitations in question may be thought of as imposed upon us by either our *sinfulness* or bad ways of thinking that have ended by leaving us trapped within *a false construction of the world*, or by *bodily existence as such*, always vulnerable and inevitably ending in old age, sickness and death.

In these last three variants our supposed captivity was described as being moral, or cognitive, or simply bodily. But these pages must have suggested to the reader that my own radical humanism could look like a state of captivity: we are always held within the limits of language, or within the limits or our humanity. We cannot escape from ourselves, or from the human world. We are always already in it, and we are never out of it.

The perception that all our post-Enlightenment critical thinking is held within limits that cannot be transcended goes back to the hard saying that 'language is only about itself'.[85] In a one-language dictionary, every word is explained in terms of other words also to be found in the same book, and so on without end. The language is a finite but endless continuum: to use the dictionary you must be already in the language, because the whole precedes the part, and of course the sideways movement from sign to sign never leads you right out of the dictionary. The world of language is outsideless, with no door leading into it, and no door leading out of it. Hence Derrida's famous line to the effect that 'there is nothing outside the text', and the Wittgenstein dictum that the limits of language are the limits of our world.

An interesting implication of this line of argument is that many of the most celebrated children's books in our language are based upon a gross intellectual error – the idea that there could be a doorway out of our ordinary human world into another order of reality. Books based upon this idea include *Alice in Wonderland, Alice through the Looking-Glass, The Chronicles of Narnia* and *His Dark Materials.* They also include *The Divine Comedy* of Dante Alighieri. But there are no holes in the world that one can step through in order to enter another quite different world, for the world is an outsideless continuum in the same way that language is. Look! There are no gaps in the visual field, and no gaps in time.

Let us now consider some of the chief views about this question of whether or not we are in some sense *imprisoned* within our human limitations.

1 The starting point must be Plato's allegory of the Cave, in the *Republic.* Here ordinary human life is compared with being chained up and immobilized in a cave, looking at pictures projected on the wall and supposing that those mere shadows are the real things to which our language refers. But, says Plato, suppose that one individual is somehow freed and induced to make his way out of the Cave and into the bright sunlight above. At first he's dazzled, but soon he sees a far better world, and learns a new and better way of using language. He is filled with pity for the deluded souls below and feels impelled to go down and rescue them, so that they too can reach the Better World above.

In this familiar story Plato is a clear metaphysical dualist, who thinks that by philosophical training we can be induced gradually to abandon a false, inadequate way of looking at the world, which stops at appearances and mistakenly takes them for granted. Instead we can gradually become habituated to a better vision of the world and a better way of using language. And this better world is the Real world.

2 Fairly close to Plato is the excellent Hollywood film, *The Truman Show* (1998, directed by Peter Weir). During the course of the film the central character gradually awakens to the realization that he has lived his entire life in a small, closed world which is 'really' the set of a long-running all-round-the-clock soap opera, a 'reality' TV show. Now this very fine film is taken by all the critics to be a satire on the power of the mass media, and especially the world of TV soaps and 'reality' shows. But the film can be read as having a much more serious purpose than that: it might be about an ordinary person's sudden sense of the spiritual emptiness, the desolate mediocrity, of ordinary small-town life, and his yearning for transcendence. He wants out. And note that within the world of the film it is possible (though very difficult) to escape.

3 In a book called *The Leap of Reason* (1976, p. 31, though I first wrote down the parable during a collaboration with L. R. Wickham as early as about 1960), I imagined someone confined in a prison without doors or windows. He has never left the prison, which (like the frog's well) is for him the world, the only world. He lives with others in this closed environment, which somehow contrives to be self-sufficient. And from this prison, unlike Plato's, there really is no way out. The inmates do not think of themselves as being confined at all: where they are is their world, their life, and they know nothing else.

I then asked the question: 'In this situation, can we imagine that one individual might be able to form the idea of "outside"? He would reason by analogy: as in self-consciousness I think myself and transcend myself, can I similarly think my whole life-situation here, and transcend it to imagine a greater world Outside all this?' The essay then went on to imagine how this restless, dissatisfied individual might struggle to amplify his concept of Outside, and might become dissatisfied with life Inside as he aspired after the Outside world.

In this early-1970s piece I was evidently halfway between naturalism and Platonism. The only way out of the Cave was by an intellectual act – 'the leap of reason' – analogous to the one involved in self-consciousness.[87] I was at that time still trying to find a new philosophical basis for theism.

4 More recently I have abandoned the inside/outside contrast when telling the following story:

Imagine that you live in an underground house. Part of the roof has fallen in, blocking the long passageway that formerly led to your usual way out. You want to leave the house, but how can you do so? You can burrow away in the soft soil in any direction you please, but all your efforts to *leave* the house can never do any more than merely *expand* it. Do you have any reason to complain that you feel imprisoned? It's not clear that you *are* imprisoned at all: for after all, your world is your world, and you can do more or less what you like within it. You can easily push out its boundaries: but you can't jump completely clear of the limits of your own troglodyte condition, and you can know nothing about any 'outside'.

To apply the metaphor, when we do natural science and enormously extend our knowledge we are not discovering new worlds, but simply pushing out the walls of the ordinary human life-world within which everybody begins. And the same is true of science-fiction and fantasy literature and cinema: they are always, if they are good dramas, stories about human relationships dressed up in fancy costumes. They are not, and cannot be stories intelligible to us about *completely non-human* but personal beings. And indeed the lesson of all epic, fantasy and science-fiction stories is the same: we can push out the boundaries of this human world of ours, but we can never entirely leave it.

So in the end there is only humanity, only the human life-world, only our language. Since it is outsideless, it's not a prison and we shouldn't moan.

5 In telling stories like 3 and 4 above I was clearly trying finally to 'get Plato's system out of mine' with the help of Wittgenstein, whose later philosophy has been called 'quietism'. That is, he tries to *cure* us of our discontent by showing us that we aren't really imprisoned at all. The universe of modern physics is finite, but unbounded. We will never come to the end or even the edge of it, so there is no useful sense in which we are 'imprisoned' inside it. 'Nothing is hidden', as Wittgenstein says: nothing is being withheld from us. Besides, we cannot even *imagine* the whole set-up being different in some major way from what we have. And the same is true of our language, and of the everyday life-world. It just is what it is, and we are free to be ourselves and to do our own thing within it.

6 Finally, there is the pessimistic philosophy of Schopenhauer, adopted by certain later writers such as Freud and Thomas Hardy. Schopenhauer was the first important European to break with the classic Western doctrine – going back to the Presocratics – that the ultimate ground of all things, whatever it be, is at least One, and is neither irrational nor unfriendly to us. No, says Schopenhauer, endless tragic conflict is at the root of everything and suffering is our fate. We can't escape it. The best we can hope for is some relief by understanding our situation, some relief from art, and final relief in the Nothingness into which we are heading. Nietzsche called this 'passive nihilism'. 'Man is a squirrel in a cage.' Nietzsche's own active nihilism accepted, in broad outline, Schopenhauer's view of reality, but affirmed that a strong individual could conquer nihilism and 'say Yes to life' by being creative. His classical, pagan kind of humanism led him to call upon us to create a new kind of human being, new gods, new myths and new values.

In summary, Schopenhauer thinks we *are* imprisoned, and is pessimistic. Nietzsche plans heroics: we can conquer nihilism by a huge effort of self-reinvention. We need to become creative on a large scale. But of course Nietzsche has no plans to go back to anything resembling Plato's vision of the world. He accepts that the Death of God has occurred and is irreversible. Indeed, he asserts that the Death of God is in the long run a very good thing, if it has the effect of allowing us to reaffirm the value of the body and this life. And Nietzsche flatly refuses to allow the suggestion that we are 'imprisoned', whether within our own humanity, or in the body, or within our own biological life, or within human limitation generally, to depress his spirits.

What about our position in this book? The background to our whole discussion is the very ancient belief that by some kind of special discipline, in philosophy or in religion, we can somehow rise above ourselves without ceasing to be ourselves, and attain a special blessedness-giving, eternal and intuitive kind of knowledge. (By the way, 'intuitive' or immediate knowledge is contrasted with *discursive* knowledge, which is dependent upon language and therefore upon time. In eternity, knowledge cannot be staged, but has to be immediate, total and simultaneous.) To this day, belief in this special, language-transcending, timeless kind of knowledge helps to fill out many people's ideas about religious experience and about life after death. In addition, Plato's idea that our ordinary everyday language is somehow amphibious, in the sense that it can be used in two entirely distinct and very different worlds, also plays a part here. In science-fiction films, aliens talk American English, many religions insist that God thinks and talks their own sacred language, and perhaps most people who believe in life after death think they'll be able to get by with English in heaven. Emanuel Swedenborg even maintained that people in heaven are segregated into different language groups!

All these ideas began to crumble with the slow rise of modern critical thinking and modern science, which from the first was sceptical about the very idea of absolute knowledge. Science and critical thinking want all knowledge to be human, corrigible and evidence-based. The new regime of truth that appealed to observation and experimental evidence was naturally impatient of hokum about shutting one's eyes and rising above sense-experience and experimental testing to an inner but 'higher' world of intuitive certainties. Instead British empiricism from Locke onwards, and critical philosophy from Kant onwards, insisted vehemently that if you plan to build a strong system of knowledge you must respect the senses and the limits of thought.

In the long run this meant that Western thought would be committed to thoroughgoing naturalism: there is only one world, everything is contingent, there's no knowledge but *human* knowledge, and all our knowledge is corrigible. And quite right too: but during the twentieth century the whole doctrine was made much stricter by the great turn to language. All 'propositional' thinking depends upon language, and the only world we have is the world to which we are given access in our language. And as language is a constantly shifting continuum within which we are immersed, so too is the world. So am I, for I too am and I live only in the daily flow of language into me and out of me.

Hence my 'Empty radical humanism', and my general acceptance of the fourth of the six positions outlined above. My life, my world, my language – all of them *with others* – all *that* is outsidelessly all there is. We need only add the late J. L. Mackie's handy summary: 'fallible knowledge and invented ethics'.

That is 'Empty radical humanism'. Alternatively, you might call it 'linguistic naturalism', or 'semiotic materialism', or 'subtle positivism', or even just 'immanence'. Is it a state of imprisonment? Not unless you can describe clearly somewhere else that we might be, and how we might get there – and *that* you can't do. No, you can't!

Now try a second question. 'Is Empty radical humanism (or whatever else you propose to call it) a sad and bleak and desperately narrow vision of the world, compared with the magnificent old religious cosmology and the Platonic metaphysics that we have lost?'

There are several answers to that. First, I am no longer sure that we have lost very much – apart from a pile of misleading anthropomorphic metaphors. Second, what we have got instead, namely the huge achievement of Western secular culture and art since the end of the Middle Ages, is surely much bigger than what we have lost. There has been an enormous expansion of human life in many directions since the late fifteenth century. And third, in this book I have been arguing that a surprising amount of religious thought and feeling has a way of coming back to us in new guises. In *The Meaning of the West*[88] I argued that the great tradition of Christian ethics continues in our own secular culture, albeit recycled under such new labels as 'liberation struggles', 'political correctness', 'socialism', 'human rights' and whatnot. Historians can easily trace these movements back to their origins in Victorian movements for social reform, and before that to Enlightenment schemes for improvement, and before that to Protestant dreams of building God's Kingdom on earth, dreams that go back to the Bible. There can be no doubt that the tradition of Christian ethics is indelible and will continue even if the old faith finally vanishes. But I have also argued that many strands of traditional religious thought and feeling are also still alive, and are helping to enrich and deepen our purely humanist and secular culture.

This claim needs further examination.

19

Hominism

The last and culminating work of Latin ecclesiastical theology was the appropriately named *Church Dogmatics* of Karl Barth (1886–1968). After a false start, Barth began the project again in 1932, and at the time of his death had published the first thirteen very large volumes of a work that remains unfinished.

Barth took his initial impetus from the pessimistic mood of Europe in the years after the First World War. After dominating the world for some three or four centuries, and after unprecedented achievements both in science and technology and in the arts, European culture appeared to have crashed. The national optimism and self-belief of the past century had been based especially upon an alliance – even a synthesis – of Christianity with human philosophy, human feeling, human religious experience, art and the belief in progress. Now there must be a divorce. Christianity needed to be purified by being restated as a purely given divine self-revelation of the One, humanly unknowable and transcendent God. This restatement must be couched not in the language of any human philosophy, but in its own terms: that is, in the vocabulary of the Bible. This means that Barth rules out any way to God through philosophy, or through conscience, or through merely human religiosity. God is to be known only on his own terms – that is, in and through Jesus Christ. Intellectually, Barth is a fideist and extremely christocentric.

The whole second millennium, now in its last century, had seen the focus of Christian attention slowly shifting from God to Christ. First-millennium Christianity had been dominated by celibate monks, Platonism and contemplative prayer. The second millennium had seen a steady shift to Christ as the model and devotional focus for the faithful believer who, Bible in hand, battled through life in this world. Now in Barth's system that growing 'christocentrism' reached its furthest extreme, sometimes described as 'christomonism'. Christ was, as it were, the Clapham Junction of Barth's system: all the lines of thought are routed through him. There was no way to what human beings need first and most of all – namely redemption of their own fallen and corrupt human nature, their reason, their conscience, their whole psychology – except through Jesus Christ. To the outward eye Jesus is a human being. He presents to us just his own – not individual, but *generic* – human nature. But his is a perfect and sinless humanity. We need it: and in it we are taught to recognize by faith the complete and definitive self-revelation of God.

Suddenly, one blinks. Barth always gives at first the impression of being an upmarket fundamentalist and an irrational dogmatist. He purports to present us with a statement of pure Christianity, completely independent of the vagaries of fashion and human culture. But suddenly one sees that Barth's 'christomonism' is really a theological version of the radical humanism that was itself also a contemporary cultural fashion. Radical humanism, of the sort that said, 'Human, we are always inside and can never get out of our own human point of view, our own human language, our own human life world, our own only-human systems of knowledge' – *that* sort of humanism in its modern form had been launched by young Hegelians such as Ludwig Feuerbach and Karl Marx. More recently, it had been well and plainly stated in a post-Darwinian context by William James and F. C. S. Schiller.[89] The first important modern linguistic philosopher, Fritz Mauthner,[90] called it 'hominism' – an anthropocentrism which is not a matter of naivety or moral weakness, but rather is the simple truth of the human situation. I've called it 'anthropomonism' in the past.

Radical humanism was, then, certainly very much around and on the map in the young Karl Barth's day. So did he know how close he was to it? In the standard Christian orthodoxy that Barth purports to be restating, Christ is not *a* man, but is generically human – that is, just 'Man' with a capital M. His generic humanity has been assumed by God's eternal Word, is individuated by the eternal divine 'person' of God's eternal Word; and is sinless. So we gain salvation by faith in Jesus Christ as God's gift of himself as Man, for us. We are offered participation in a new and sinless humanity that God in Christ has personally assumed and road-tested for our sakes.

So now the position seems to be as follows: Barth accesses everything – salvation, eternal life, and then the regeneration of human reason, conscience, and the rest – *everything*, through the sinless generic humanity that is manifest in Christ: whereas the ordinary modern radical humanist accesses everything, *really* everything, via the generically human; that is, through human language, the human life-world and the human point of view, which are all we'll ever have, and all we need. What's the difference? One is bound to suspect that the difference is only 'spin': Barth couches his message in the traditional Latin Christian vocabulary. He uses all the right passwords and presses all the right buttons. Like all successful theologians, he is skilled in disguise and distraction. But nowadays we have all read our Nietzsche and we all know the score.

The true position, then, is as follows: Barth's christomonism was the last ecclesiastical theology and anthropomonism is the first post-ecclesiastical theology, the two differing by about the thickness of a sheet of paper. But perhaps Barth himself never entertained such thoughts. At the end of his career he was even ready to compromise his own original principles and risk a more humanistic vocabulary, especially in the short book *The Humanity of God* (1961). But if he is willing to see that, on his own account, in Christ as God's self-revelation to us God and generic humanity effectively *coincide*, then he really should have seen that it would take only one puff of wind to blow down his house of theological cards and leave only radical humanism.

Certainly it is notable that during that same decade of the 1960s a number of the keenest radical theologians who came out of the woodwork were suddenly demythologized Barthians. They were people who had belatedly grasped how profound is Christianity's inner drive towards secular humanism, from the preaching of the historical Jesus onwards.[91] That is the nerve of Christianity's power to liberate human beings: it frees us from the slavery of the law – that is, heteronomous religion. It frees us even from itself; or at least, from the Church. Anthropomonism is, after all, not a 'prison': it is pure human *freedom*.

Furthermore, as we have seen during the course of the present book, thoroughgoing anthropomonism or hominism reflexively recoils upon itself and demythologizes itself. We realize how inadequate, corrigible and only-human are all our ideas about *ourselves*. We too are constructed within the language that flows in and out of us every day. So we cannot be in danger of divinizing ourselves: on the contrary, we need to point out that Wordsworth *did* use somewhat over-grandiose language about 'the mind of man', and we should take care to avoid that kind of inflation ourselves. If we do this, then we may be surprised by the amount of traditional religious symbolism, feeling and thought that can and does return to us in new forms.

For how long has our culture been secular-humanist? The old sort of humanism that said 'Man is the measure of all things' existed in classical antiquity, and there were again a few such people in Renaissance times. But in Britain awareness that in the metropolitan cities[92] a whole class of people (roughly, the young gentleman-amateur 'wits' from whom the Deists came, and for whom they wrote) has appeared, and are now saying with impunity that they reject the standard preacher's appeal to revelation, mystery and authority, and that in their view the received orthodox theology is incredible – this awareness first developed in the last years of the seventeenth century. Another way of dating it is to examine the rise and the growing popularity of the novel – secular prose fiction. Look at the gulf between Bunyan and Defoe: they are not many years apart, but they live in very different worlds.[93] The Toleration Act of 1689, followed by the publication of John Locke's *Letters Concerning Toleration* (1690), helped to create a new climate in which clerical intellectuals such as Swift and Joseph Butler could feel that the Church was on the defensive. They might ridicule the Deists and freethinkers, but they could not check their influence, nor the gradual spread of an habitually secular mentality.

Swift in 1708 published an entertainingly ironical tract against the young 'wits': *An Argument to Prove that the Abolishing of Christianity may ... be attended with some Inconveniences.*[94] He raises the question of whether the abolition of Christianity may perhaps endanger the Church? Not for the present, answers Swift reassuringly, but in the long run the repeal of the Christian religion could be a 'step towards altering the Constitution of the Church Established, and setting up *Presbytery* in the stead'.[95]

Swift's reassurances have been justified by the event. A century later, in Jane Austen's six novels the whole apparatus of advowsons, benefice incomes and the social position of the clergy as respectable minor gentry (and possible husbands) remains mercifully intact, long after Christianity has entirely vanished as a topic of conversation. Emma once exclaims 'Good God!', but I think there may be no other use of the words 'God' or 'Christ' in the entire canon. Today, after another two centuries the Constitution remains largely unreformed, Bishops still sit *ex officio* in the House of Lords, and the Church remains as unable as ever to reconcile itself to the modern 'critical' kind of thinking. By being obstinately conservative and by sliding slowly and gently downmarket, the Church has proved able to prolong its own life for centuries. And what else does it exist for? In Britain most, if not all, of our many ancient institutions have ended by existing only in order to prolong their own existence, and we don't seem to worry about it. But I have now finally decided that it is much too late to think of reforming the Church, and that we can spend our time much more profitably in looking at and thinking about what is developing in the post-Christian culture outside the Church.

In Jane Austen's world, and also in the worlds of Mrs Gaskell and Dickens a generation or two later, Christian doctrinal beliefs may have entirely vanished from the world of everyday life, but Christian humanitarian ethics is becoming steadily stronger and more active. As I have argued elsewhere,[96] the best traditions of Christian ethics remain in surprisingly good health, and we are not likely to abandon them. No doubt the reason for this is that Christian humanitarian ethics derives historically from the markedly humanist outlook and teaching of Jesus himself. It is logically quite independent of the Church's supernatural doctrines, and therefore can happily survive their demise.

What of the larger scene? It is rather like a return of sixth-century England: around us we see everywhere the remains of a once-great civilization, now falling into ruin. A few ultra-conservatives are still operating among the ruins, trying to pretend that they can keep the show going just a little longer; and other 'fundamentalists' seem to think that they still possess 'the essence of Christianity' and may even be able to restore its former glory. But it cannot be done. Their religion is desperately reduced – much more so than they realize – and the attempt to *force* oneself to believe such things today produces a sadly damaged psychology. Not to mention dreadfully bad writing and art.

All the same things are true of the two or three other major 'world religions' that still survive and have a little vitality left within them. Their 'great' periods all ended around 1800, or even somewhat earlier, and cannot now be recovered. The impact of 'the West' – that is, critical thinking, science and technology, globalization and radical humanism – has simply swept aside and made obsolete all earlier world-views, despite the protestations of many to the contrary.

An example: Islam came into its maturity quicker than any other major tradition, and produced what was in its day an

integrated and beautiful social order, housed in superb architecture across the whole range of building types. No other
faith has, in its heyday and by the standards of those times,
been so successful in building a total and harmonious society.
Inevitably, there are those who still think it may be possible
to build a modern version of the Islamic state, as good today
as the old order was then. But alas, times have changed so
much that it is not going to be done.

Another example: the special excellence of Christianity (and
also Judaism) was chiefly in 'micropolitics', that is, the ethics
of personal relationships. (Ecclesiastical Christianity never
purported to be able to build a complete and integrated religious society on this earth, and the Church nowhere simply
coincided with the State.) Today, the old ethical tradition still
continues, but its best achievements are rather recent, and
have depended upon its gradual self-dissociation from the
Church. Consider, for example, the emancipation of women
and homosexuals, and the developing ethical codes of the
learned professions and of public service. In all these areas it
has been expedient to break away from the Church, which no
longer needs to be consulted.

It is this observation, that the best surviving strands in
the Christian tradition have now largely left the Churches,
that has often led me to argue that our efforts at reconstruction should now take the form of a *consciously post-
ecclesiastical* 'Kingdom theology'. In order to rejuvenate
Christianity, we need to move it on a whole 'dispensation',
or historical epoch.

In this present book we have introduced a further set of
considerations. Although our dominant culture has been
secular-humanist for two (or even for three) centuries now, a
surprising variety of traditional forms of religious experience
and doctrinal themes do seem to be returning to us in fresh
guises. Perhaps we should be systematically collecting up this
material, and seeing whether something new and interesting
can perhaps be built out of it?

20

Conclusions

Our culture has been predominantly secular-humanist for two or three centuries – briefly, for the period during which the novel has been the most important and popular literary genre. To put it in terms of English literature, Bunyan's *Mr Badman* (1680) is still religious tract rather than true prose fiction, and Swift's *Gulliver's Travels* (1726) is the work not of a novelist, but a satirist; whereas Defoe's *Robinson Crusoe* (1719) can be called our first true novel. Thereafter the novel developed rapidly, until in the hands of someone like Samuel Richardson it could begin to justify Iris Murdoch's description of it as 'our best totalizing medium'. The mainstream novel shows us the human heart, and shows us our life as it is – and the human life-world it shows us is a world that has become completely secular. In more recent years the same has been true of drama, cinema and broadcasting. Even in the United States, where such a surprisingly high proportion of the population remains professedly religious, mainstream cinema is notably secular.

Today we live in a culture that has long been secular-humanist, but many people are strongly religious in temperament, and we are surrounded by reminders of the old faith that we have now almost entirely lost. Of special interest are the occasions when we notice a traditional religious idea or theme returning in a new and strange guise, and it was such occasions that were the starting point for this book. I wanted to ask: 'How far can religious thought and feeling survive, whether encapsulated or in modified form, within a completely secular culture? And what about the latest form of our secularity, postmodernism?' Postmodernity is completely without any Platonism, or 'metaphysics'. In it nothing is primary, nothing is foundational, nothing is absolute or objective. On the contrary, everything is fleeting, 'relative' and ambivalent. It is a phenomenalism of the sign. Yet even in postmodernism there are still very strong religious echoes, like the crucifix in Damien Hirst, and the free use of religious language by Jeff Koons. What does it all amount to?

In the preceding chapters we have discussed this question, and now it is time to draw the threads together. What have we got?

Our first and most important finding is that we may now be ready for the return of (a new kind of) Grand Narrative theology. The old Western Grand Narrative was finally killed off at the end of the seventeenth century, when the triumph of Newton marked the end of the old control of cosmology by religion. But ever since then we have felt the need to tell a great story about how we came to be what we now are, and how we got here. Why was religious belief so necessary to us for so very long, and why have we somehow lost it? Recent developments in archaeology and anthropology suggest a returning confidence that it may after all be possible to reconstruct something of the early history of 'the human mind' (or, as I prefer to call it, 'our ideal culture'). I think we are now ready for such a theory, and have tried to indicate the form it might take. In a much reprinted paper of 1964, 'Religious Evolution', Robert N. Bellah[97] made one of the very few recent attempts to sketch such a theory, but few have followed him. When we have such a theory, it will change the way we see religion, our old nurse, and we will find it easier to be reconciled to our own lost tradition, to love it, and even to make some use of it again.

Our second – and perhaps equally important – finding is that we may at last be able to reconnect *cosmos* and *ethos*, our world-picture and our ethic. During the twentieth century we gradually learnt to abandon the old religious *and Newtonian* notion that the cosmos is a stable created order, and replace it with a new picture of the cosmos as a vast slow-motion explosion, pouring out and passing away, and in its long slow process giving rise here and there to fabulous beauties and complexities. In a post-metaphysical age this may suggest a new placing of the word 'God': we should see God not as a substance, a super-being who creates once and for all, but as continuously self-outpouring be-ing, coming out into actuality through our language. God is his own burning and dying: he is always passing away. Back to Heraclitus.

In ethics, there has been a corresponding shift. We have learnt to give up the old ideas of unchanging and objective moral laws, or essences, or standards, and instead are coming to see ethics in 'solar' terms. Just as there is no permanent and objective real world out there, so also there is no permanent and objective moral order out there. Instead, there is only an outpouring and passing away that is given meaning and value for us by the language in which we briefly fix it. Thus ethics becomes more subjective, emotive, human and expressivist: it becomes a shifting, pouring-out and passing-away ethics of *love*, 'solar living'. Jesus of Nazareth, surprisingly, actually taught such an ethic, associating it with imagery of light and the sun; which is why we may become able again to see him as linking ethos and cosmos, morality and nature. Here we see the possibility of a certain return of the old faith, or at least, of some major themes in it. But we must get rid of the old doctrine system and the institutions linked to it, before we can see and get hold of the new.

Third, in our discussion we have seen the return, in a new and more worldly guise, of a number of traditional divine attributes and operations. The creative power of God's Word returns (Introduction, and Chapter 2) in our modern recognition of the active, performative uses of language. The grace of God returns in our modern recognition of the utter gratuitousness of our life and its joys (Chapter 9). The divine life returns in our modern awareness of life as continually springing up within us; and as being all around us the outsideless totality within which we ourselves live and move and have our being (Chapter 4). The divine light or Glory returns to us in our own recognition of the conscious 'brightness' and exhilaration of visual experience (Chapter 5). The divine power and greatness returns to us in our own vivid awe at and enjoyment of the sublime in Nature (Chapter 11). The divine scrutiny and judgement upon us returns to us in a new 'internalized' form, as we fully assimilate the modern critical and *self*-critical way of thinking (Chapter 8). And most of all, we ourselves are God's most important legacy: he taught us everything, and has recently died finally to complete our education (Chapter 17).

In summary, we need not complain that the late Modern radical-humanist world-view is very meagre and barren. It can still be irradiated with vivid religious feeling – and much more so than you think. Eternal life or beatitude can return to us also, in the Now-moment (Chapter 15), and the cosmic, regnant Christ can return to us in our modern radical humanism (Chapter 10).

It thus appears that even within a radical-humanist, and *even within a postmodern*, world-view rather more of Christianity can return than we used to think. In another recent book I have argued that the original, historical Jesus – a man who lived imaginatively at the end of the world – was actually a teacher of the kind of 'solar living' that is the ethic appropriate to our own world-view. Is it then possible that there might in time be a second Reformation of the Church along these lines?

I fear not. We would be talking about a much bigger Reformation than the sixteenth-century one, and it would involve the end of the Church in anything like its present form. But the Church, like other major religious traditions, regards its own faith as final. It already knows the fullness of truth and has nothing to learn. And I must confess that (with only one or two exceptions) New Testament scholars are showing little enthusiasm for my reconstruction of Jesus' original message. So I doubt if we can talk of a new Reformation. But the religious ideas and feelings that have been described here will continue, and will continue to be a great consolation. Remember that, apart from them, our life after its early peak leaves us with little to look forward to except the long downward slope to extinction. It helps to be regularly distracted by a few moments, or even hours, of eternal happiness here and there, and it helps to practise living-by-dying.

Appendix

A Note on Humanism

Like 'Nature', 'humanism' is a word with a long history that has been appropriated by many different people for use in many different senses.

The first important philosophical humanist was Protagoras of Abdera (*c.* 490–*c.* 421 BCE), one of the Sophists and the author of the saying, 'Man is the measure of all things.' He was both anthropocentric and individualistic, holding that you should be true to yourself, and that truth is what is true for you. Thus in effect he denied objective knowledge and objective Truth, and was a thoroughgoing relativist. Sadly, no work by him survives, but one of Plato's dialogues bears his name.

In the Old Testament (and especially in Psalm 8) we find a different kind of humanism. Under God, man has been allotted a special place in the cosmic order: he has one foot in the visible world, where he is the crown of creation; and the other foot in the supernatural world into which God co-opts him. This vision of the 'middle state' of man had a very long history, the last full and notable statement of it being Alexander Pope's, in his *Essay on Man*:

Know then thyself, presume not God to scan;
The proper study of mankind is man.
Placed on this isthmus of a middle state,
A being darkly wise and rudely great;
With too much knowledge for the sceptic side,
With too much weakness for the stoic's pride,
He hangs between, in doubt to act or rest;
In doubt to deem himself a god or beast;

In doubt his mind or body to prefer;
Born but to die, and reasoning but to err . . .

Great lord of all things, yet a prey to all;
Sole judge of truth, in endless error hurled;
The glory, jest and riddle of the world!

A third kind of humanist is *literary*. Whereas theologians study 'sacred letters' – that is, Scripture and texts related to it – a humanist is a person who studies 'human letters' – that is, the secular writers of Greek and Roman antiquity. The tradition of literary humanists begins with the writers of the fourteenth-century Italian Renaissance and runs up to Erasmus, Colet and More in the England of King Henry VIII.

What I call 'radical humanism' stems from the work of Hume and Kant, the philosophers who made the most important attempts to explain what human knowledge is *without* invoking God's absolute power and knowledge to back it up, or justify it. For this kind of humanist, we are on our own, and always have been. We alone invented our language: nobody taught it to us. We alone invented all our knowledge: nobody dictated any of it to us. Nothing other than ourselves teaches us, or corrects or validates our efforts. It follows that we are in no position to distinguish between *our* world (the world as it appears to us) and *the* world (the world as it is absolutely). On the contrary, we must recognize and accept that we are always inside our only-human vision of the world, and cannot ever jump clear of it. It seems to follow that we ought to be pragmatists, who regard as true those beliefs that we have found to work satisfactorily for us and which survive the tests we devise for them.

In the great tradition of modern German philosophy that stems from Kant and Hegel this kind of humanism is always called Idealism. For philosophical idealists, our thinking 'conditions' or shapes whatever we think about, so that mind and reality are always interwoven. Truth is therefore not primarily a matter of *correspondence* between a mental representation and a material state of affairs, but of the *coherence* of the whole, the evolving totality.

Since the heyday of German Idealism the terms have shifted somewhat. Instead of saying that the world is shaped by the a priori *categories of the human understanding* (Kant), people will say that our vision of the world is shaped by our *culture* (Durkheim), or by our *language* (Benjamin Whorf, and linguistic philosophy since the 1930s).

Against this background, I should now say that my own radical humanism was shaped by my early exposure to Hume and Kant, and by the fact that my first philosophy teacher (N. R. Hanson) introduced me to Wittgenstein's thought in the year 1953–54, before the *Philosophical Investigations* was published. It is a fact: radical humanism *is* rather close to Idealism, even though in Britain people are wary of the term, and prefer to describe Wittgenstein's position as 'linguistic naturalism', and Derrida's as 'semiotic materialism'.

Notes

1 In his *A Treatise of Human Nature* (1739–40), Book One.

2 I introduced the contrast between 'heterological' and 'autological' thinking in *The Old Creed and the New*, London: SCM Press, 2006.

3 See my *Impossible Loves*, Santa Rosa: Polebridge Press, 2007.

4 From his ode to music 'On St Cecilia's Day' (1687).

5 'World' is etymologically 'wer-uld', the age a man lives in.

6 In the old volume of Hegel's *Early Theological Writings* look up the opening pages of *The Spirit of Christianity and Its Fate* (1798), and especially the treatment of Noah, caught in a storm at sea.

7 Q/Luke 12.57.

8 *Thomas* 14.5; Mark 15.10–11. Cited from Robert W. Funk, *The Gospel of Jesus* 14:7, Santa Rosa: Polebridge Press, 1999, p. 67.

9 Psalm 82.6, cited in John 10.34.

10 Recent scholarship dates the editing of the Hebrew Bible much later than the older critical orthodoxy did, so that we may nowadays recognize a good deal of Platonic influence upon the Hebrew text.

11 Wordsworth (despite his tendency to nature-worship) and Shelley (despite his atheism) are both still clearly influenced by Plato in their use of the words eternal and eternity.

12 *Blake: Complete Writings*, ed. Geoffrey Keynes, Oxford University Press, many editions, 'Poems and Fragments from the Notebook, written about 1793', nos. 43, 59; pp. 179, 184.

13 From the very fine little group of 'Eternity' poems, written in the Northampton Asylum in the 1840s.

14 The Latin adjective *clarus* has similar associations: think of its cognates, such as 'clarify' and 'declare'.

15 J. B. Pritchard, *Ancient Near-Eastern Texts Relating to the Old Testament*, 3rd edn, Princeton, NJ: Princeton University Press, 1969, pp. 3–7.

16 There is a modern edition by J. I. Cope and H. W. Jones, 1959.

17 From *His Majesty's Declaration*, 1628, prefixing the English Thirty-Nine Articles of Religion.

18 In the Hebrew numbering, see for example Psalms 105, 106, 107, 136.

19 Especially in Romans.

20 The New Zealand philosopher and historian of ideas John Passmore could still publish a big book on this topic as late as 1970 (London, Duckworth); but today it is suddenly quite forgotten.

21 As witness the well-known works of writers such as C. S. Lewis, J. R. R. Tolkien and Philip Pullman.

22 *You Can't Go Home Again*, by Thomas Clayton Wolfe (1900–38), first published posthumously in 1940.

23 An early essay by Jacques Derrida, 'Edmond Jabès and the Question of the book', reprinted in his *Writing and Difference* is the classic postmodern critique of this idea of the totalizing Book. The best satires against the Book are Sterne's *Tristram Shandy* and Flann O'Brien's *At Swim-Two-Birds*. The thesis that 'the postmodern condition' consists in scepticism about all Grand Narratives was classically advanced by J.-F. Lyotard, especially in *La Condition Postmoderne* (Paris: Minuit, 1979; ET, Manchester University Press, 1984).

24 See for example *The Old Creed and the New*, London: SCM Press, 2006, and especially chs 18 and 22. The idea of creating a new kind of Grand Narrative in the form of a history of human thought *purely from the inside* begins (over-ambitiously) with Hegel's *Phenomenology of Spirit*, and continues, in a more chastened form, in Nietzsche, Heidegger, Vattimo and others. It has haunted me for years, despite the very sharp criticisms to which anyone who tries to think himself into the minds of other humans long ago and far away is obviously exposing himself. In this present book I indulge myself.

25 Ross Wilson, *Subjective Universality in Kant's Aesthetics*, Bern: Peter Lang AG, 2007, ch. 4, 'Feeling, Life and the Feeling of Life', pp. 109–46.

26 Ross Wilson (ed.), *The Meaning of 'Life' in Romantic Poetry and Poetics*, London and New York: Routledge, 2009.

27 L. A. Feuerbach's *The Essence of Christianity*, 1841, was translated into English by the young George Eliot, 1854, and has influenced all English-language radical theology since.

28 *Blake: Complete Writings*, cited above, n. 12, 'The Everlasting Gospel', see pp. 752f.

29 Beginning with *The New Religion of Life in Everyday Speech*, London: SCM Press, 1999.

30 *The Meaning of the West*, London: SCM Press, 2008. In this thesis (that Christian ecclesiastical theology is dead, but Christian culture is still very much alive and developing), I am close to the ideas of

the New Zealander Lloyd Geering, who has been advancing the same thesis for at least three decades.

31 See my *Mysticism After Modernity*, Malden, MA and Oxford: Blackwell 1998, and also Deuteronomy 30.20 (RV): God 'is thy life and thy length of days'.

32 I cite Henry Vaughan from *The Metaphysical Poets*, ed. Helen Gardner, Harmondsworth: Penguin Books, 1957, p. 269.

33 Vaughan, in *The Metaphysical Poets*, p. 263.

34 Vaughan, in *The Metaphysical Poets*, p. 278.

35 Vaughan, in *The Metaphysical Poets*, p. 279.

36 *William Wordsworth: The Major Works*, ed. with an Introduction and Notes Stephen Gill, Oxford University Press, 1984, paperback version with revisions, 2000, pp. 297–302. Always use this edition for the study of Wordsworth's thought.

37 *William Wordsworth*, ed. Gill, p. 714.

38 *William Wordsworth*, ed. Gill, p. 714.

39 *William Wordsworth*, ed. Gill, p. 714.

40 'Home at Grasmere', ll. 1006–14, in *William Wordsworth*, ed. Gill, p. 198. Gill thinks that these lines belong to the year 1806.

41 *Leviathan*, 1651.

42 For example, E. B. Tylor, *Primitive Culture*, 1871. Tylor's discussion includes good comments about the 'blocks to falsifiability' which keep people clinging to traditional beliefs in the absence of any evidence for their truth and efficacy.

43 I have told this story in various slightly different ways at different times. See for example *The Old Creed and the New*, London; SCM Press, 2006, ch. 22.

44 See John S. Kloppenborg and others, *Q-Thomas Reader*, Sonoma, CA: Polebridge Press, 1990, p. 64. Kloppenborg evidently reckons that this remarkable sentence is part of Q. The Jesus Seminar considered that it was invented by Luke to provide a lead-in for verses 58f., which they designated pink. See Robert W. Funk, Roy W. Hoover et al., *The Five Gospels*, New York: Scribner, 1996, p. 344. Kierkegaard liked the saying enough to use it as a book title, *Judge for Yourselves!* (Funk's translation: 'Why can't you decide for yourselves what is right?'), but neither Kierkegaard nor any modern New Testament critics have ever yet seen how radical Jesus' challenge is – if indeed the words be his.

45 Genesis 3, 17, 21–24.

46 In Greek *Archē* means beginning, first cause, origin.

47 There is in Methodism a very interesting strain of ecstatic radical humanism which is close to my own point of view. See for example the Wesley hymn, 'O thou who camest from above'. It closely echoes the mood of these paragraphs.

48 *Jesus and Philosophy*, London: SCM Press, 2009, provides the basis in the teaching of Jesus for a new Christianity along these lines.

49 It seems to have been Wittgenstein who first saw Kierkegaard as a non-realist – no doubt, because of the influence of Kant upon him. But the whole subject is controversial.

50 'To a Louse'.

51 Luke 18.9–14; 13.14–15.

52 In *Jesus and Philosophy*, I see Jesus as an important pioneer of critical thinking in ethics (and, therefore, of course as having been much more radical in theology than has hitherto been supposed).

53 See my *The Meaning of the West*, London: SCM Press, 2008.

54 For the words being discussed here, see *The Religion of Being*, London: SCM Press, 1998, ch. 4.

55 I am much indebted here to the writings of Steven Mithen, starting (for me) with his essay in Colin Renfrew and Ezra B. W. Zubrow, *The Ancient Mind: Elements of Cognitive Archaeology*, Cambridge University Press, 1994, pp. 29–39. Of course much depends on the dating of the origin of language, which seems to be still up in the air.

56 Giant humans include Adam in some intertestamental Jewish writings, the 'Perfect Man' in early Islamic mysticism, and the colossal images of Christ and of the Buddha that are well known. The giant size of these figures may indicate a human perfection, now lost, that is to be reattained in the future.

57 See my *Jesus and Philosophy*.

58 Luther Link, *The Devil*, London: Reaktion Books, 1995, plate 64. The book contains a useful history of Satan.

59 Henry-Russell Hitchcock, *Rococo Architecture in Southern Germany*, London: Phaidon Press, 1968.

60 2 Kings 3.13–15.

61 For example Colossians 1.15.

62 *William Wordsworth*, ed. Gill, p. 281. Caroline was born on 15 December 1793, and therefore still aged eight in August 1802.

63 *William Wordsworth*, ed. Gill, pp. xx.

64 Abridged from the closing lines of the *Prelude*, in *William Wordsworth*, ed. Gill, pp. 589f.

65 Patrick L. Gardiner (ed.), *Nineteenth-Century Philosophy*, New York: Free Press, 1969, p. 25.

66 For example, Thérèse of Lisieux and Mother Teresa of Calcutta.

67 John Milbank is perhaps most fairly described as a neo-Augustinian.

68 For example in *The Old Creed and the New* and in *Jesus and Philosophy*.

69 Genesis 3.5.

70 Some argue that a new geological epoch, the 'Anthropocene', has just begun. It is the period dominated by the rapid growth of humankind towards spectacular self-destruction.

71 Sartre may have influenced Foucault here, even though the latter would have denied it vigorously.

72 For an earlier account on these lines of the religion of the future, see my *After God*, London: Weidenfeld and Nicolson, 1997, ch. 12. Wittgenstein took a rather similar line.

73 One of the very best is in the Fitzwilliam Museum at Cambridge; another is in the Victoria and Albert Museum, London.

74 For example, in the closing lines of the *Prelude*.

75 W. E. Hoskins and Oliver Rackham (the author of *A History of the Countryside*) are among those who have most effectively taught the public that one can read the countryside's history as easily and profitably as an architectural historian reads a city.

76 I am indebted to Colin Renfrew, Steven Mithen and the 'cognitive archaeologists' for prompting me to think about the early human mind, a topic I have hoped for decades to be able to address one day.

77 The reference is to *Ancient Evenings*, on which Mailer toiled for ten years. The literary critics panned it. Ancient prephilosophical thought has been made accessible by a small number of authors and books, including the old classic H. Frankfort (ed.), *The Intellectual Adventure of Ancient Man*, Chicago: University of Chicago Press, 1941, and Thorkild Jacobsen, *The Treasures of Darkness*, New Haven: Yale University Press, 1976.

78 In English seventeenth-century poetry, allegory takes the form of a debate between, for example, soul and body, or the philosopher and the lover.

79 *Jesus and Philosophy*.

80 *Jesus and Philosophy* was a little too delicately phrased for people to be able to grasp its real message, and in what follows I am being a little more explicit.

81 Jeremiah 31.33; Ezekiel 11.19; 36.26, etc.

82 Among more recent writers, William Blake comes perhaps nearest to understanding Jesus here. See Christopher Rowland's forthcoming book.

83 Elisabeth Dahnens, *Hubert and Jan Van Eyck*, © Mercaterfonds of Antwerp; published in the UK by Alpine Fine Arts, n.d.

84 See my *The Great Questions of Life*, Santa Rosa, CA: Polebridge Press, 2005.

85 '. . . a real conversation is just a game of words. One can only be amazed at the ridiculous mistake, that people think they speak

for the sake of things. Of the fact that language is peculiar because it only concerns itself with itself, nobody is aware . . .' Novalis, *Monologue* (1798), cited in Andrew Bowie, *From Romanticism to Critical Theory*, London and New York: Routledge, 1995, p. 65.

86 At the beginning of Book VII, 514–16.

87 Influenced by Kierkegaard, I guess. I still believed in something like a substantial self until about 1985.

88 London: SCM Press, 2008.

89 Ferdinand Canning Scott Schiller (1864–1937) was very close in outlook to William James. See his *Humanism* (1912). He taught at Oxford, and in his later years at the University of Southern California.

90 Gershom Weiler, *Mauthner's Critique of Language*, Cambridge University Press, 1970.

91 See my *Jesus and Philosophy*. The message of this book, that Jesus' preaching implied the Death of God, was missed by readers. In fact, Jesus' critique of ethical heteronomy, and his insistence that moral judgements are not truly moral at all unless they spring from our own hearts *alone*, makes his preaching clearly 'blasphemous' by the standards of his own day.

92 That is, principally London, Edinburgh and perhaps Dublin.

93 Daniel Defoe was born in about 1660, but his famous novels were written rather late in his life: *Robinson Crusoe* appeared in 1719, and *Moll Flanders* in 1722.

94 John Hayward (ed.), *Swift: Gulliver's Travels and Selected Writings in Prose and Verse*, London: Nonesuch Press, and New York: Random House, 1949.

95 Hayward (ed.), *Swift*, p. 394.

96 In *The Meaning of the West*, cited above, n. 53.

97 *American Sociological Review*, vol. 29, pp. 358–74.

Bibliography and Further Reading

I list here only books expressly referred to in the text and notes, specifying the editions from which I have quoted.

Augustine, *The City of God*, trans. Henry Bettenson, Harmondsworth: Pelican Books, 1972.

Karl Barth, *The Humanity of God*, London: Collins, 1961.

—— *Church Dogmatics*, Edinburgh: T. & T. Clark, 1958–.

William Blake, *Complete Writings*, ed. Geoffrey Keynes, Oxford: Oxford University Press, many editions.

John Clare, *Poems of John Clare's Madness*, ed. Geoffrey Grigson, London: Routledge and Kegan Paul, 1949.

Don Cupitt, *After God*, New York: Basic Books, London: Weidenfeld and Nicolson, 1997.

—— *The Religion of Being*, London: SCM Press, 1998.

—— *The New Religion of Life in Everyday Speech*, London: SCM Press, 1999.

—— *The Old Creed and the New*, London: SCM Press, 2006.

—— *Impossible Loves*, Santa Rosa, CA: Polebridge Press, 2007.

—— *Above Us Only Sky*, Santa Rosa, CA; Polebridge Press, 2008.

—— *The Meaning of the West*, London: SCM Press, 2008.

—— *Jesus and Philosophy*, London: SCM Press, 2009.

Jacques Derrida, *Writing and Difference*, trans. Alan Bass, London and New York: Routledge, 1978.

John Dryden, *Poetry, Prose and Plays*, ed. Douglas Grant, London: Rupert Hart-Davis, 1952.

Meister Eckhart, *A New Translation*, by R. B. Blakney, New York: Harper Torchbooks, 1957.

Ludwig Feuerbach, *The Essence of Christianity*, trans. George Eliot, London, 1854.

H. Frankfort (ed.), *The Intellectual Adventure of Ancient Man*, Chicago: University of Chicago Press, 1941.

Robert W. Funk, Roy Hoover and Others, *The Five Gospels*, New York: Scribner, 1996.

BIBLIOGRAPHY AND FURTHER READING

Patrick L. Gardiner (ed.), *Nineteenth-Century Philosophy*, New York: Free Press, 1969.

Helen Gardner, *The Metaphysical Poets*, Harmondsworth: Penguin Books, 1957.

G. W. F. Hegel, *The Spirit of Christianity and Its Fate* (1998), repr. in *Hegel: Early Theological Writings*, trans. T. M. Knox, Chicago: University of Chicago Press, 1948.

Henry Russell Hitchcock, *Rococo Architecture in Southern Germany*, London: Phaidon Press, 1968.

Thomas Hobbes, *Leviathan*, 1651.

David Hume, *A Treatise of Human Nature*, 1739–40; ed. L. A. Selby-Bigge, Oxford: Oxford University Press, 1941, etc.

Thorkild Jacobsen, *The Treasures of Darkness*, New Haven, CN: Yale University Press, 1976.

Immanual Kant, *The Critique of Judgement*, 1790.

Søren Kierkegaard, *Purity of Heart is to Will One Thing*, Copenhagen, 1846.

John S. Kloppenborg and others, *Q-Thomas Reader*, Sonoma, CA: Polebridge Press, 1990.

Luther Link, *The Devil*, London: Reacktion Books, 1995.

Jean-François Lyotard, *The Postmodern Condition*, Paris, 1979; ET, Manchester University Press, 1984.

Norman Mailer, *Ancient Evenings*, London: Macmillan, 1983.

Isaac Newton, *Philosophiae Naturalis Principia Mathematica*, 1687.

John Passmore, *The Perfectibility of Man*, London: Duckworth, 1970.

J. B. Pritchard, *Ancient Near-Eastern Texts relating to the Old Testament*, 3rd edn, Princeton, NJ: Princeton University Press, 1969.

Oliver Rackham, *The History of the Countryside*, London: J. M. Dent, 1986.

Colin Renfrew and Ezra B. W. Zubrow, *The Ancient Mind: Elements of Cognitive Archaeology*, Cambridge University Press, 1994.

Thomas Sprat, *History of the Royal Society*, 1667.

Jonathan Swift, *Gulliver's Travels and Selected Writings in Prose and Verse*, London: Nonesuch Press, and New York: Random House, 1949.

Edward B. Tylor, *Primitive Culture*, 1871.

Gershon Weiler, *Mauthner's Critique of Language*, Cambridge University Press, 1970.

Ross Wilson, *Subjective Universality in Kant's Aesthetics*, Bern: Peter Lang AG, 2007.

—— *The Meaning of Life in Romantic Poetry and Poetics*, London and New York: Routledge, 2009.

Thomas Wolfe, *You Can't Go Home Again*, 1940.

William Wordsworth, *The Major Works*, ed. Stephen Gill, Oxford: Oxford University Press, 2000.

Index